CRE▲TIVE
HOMEOWNER®

# design ideas for
# Fireplaces

CREATIVE HOMEOWNER®, Upper Saddle River, New Jersey

# CRE𝐀TIVE HOMEOWNER®

A Division of Federal Marketing Corp.
Upper Saddle River, NJ

**DESIGN IDEAS FOR FIREPLACES**
SENIOR EDITOR: Kathie Robitz
SENIOR DESIGNER: Glee Barre
GRAPHIC DESIGNER: Susan Johnston
PHOTO EDITOR: Stan Sudol
JUNIOR GRAPHIC DESIGNER: Maureen Mulligan
EDITORIAL ASSISTANT: Jennifer Calvert (proofreading)
INDEXER: Schroeder Indexing Services
FRONT COVER PHOTOGRAPHY: (center) www.davidduncanlivingston.com (bottom left)courtesy of Vermont Castings; (bottom center and bottom right) Jessie Walker
INSIDE FRONT COVER PHOTOGRAPHY: (top) courtesy of Vermont Castings;
    (bottom) courtesy of Linex
BACK COVER PHOTOGRAPHY: (top, bottom right, and bottom left) Jessie Walker;
    (bottom center) Mark Lohman
INSIDE BACK COVER PHOTOGRAPHY: (top) Jessie Walker; (bottom) courtesy of Boulder
  Creek

**CREATIVE HOMEOWNER**
VP/PUBLISHER: Timothy O. Bakke
PRODUCTION DIRECTOR: Kimberly H. Vivas
ART DIRECTOR: David Geer
MANAGING EDITOR: Fran J. Donegan

Printed in China

Current Printing (last digit)
10 9 8 7 6 5 4 3 2 1
Design Ideas for Fireplaces, First Edition
Library of Congress Control Number: 2007923036
ISBN-10: 1-58011-363-X
ISBN-13: 978-1-58011-363-2

CREATIVE HOMEOWNER®
A Division of Federal Marketing Corp.
24 Park Way
Upper Saddle River, NJ 07458
**www.creativehomeowner.com**

# Dedication

This book is dedicated to my parents, H. Roy and Beverly Lamansky, who provided their seven children with a living example of how we can do anything we strive for. And, to the Good Lord for giving me the physiological capability to pursue challenges. Also for the gift of my grandson Skye, who gives me the desire and ambition to leave my footprint in life's pathway.

Thanks goes to those who supported me during this project, especially my sisters, sisters-in-law and brothers, other family and friends including my co-workers at Harper Brush, Inc., especially my other "family" in Marketing.

I owe a huge debt of gratitude to Barry Harper, CEO of Harper Brush Works, Inc., who allowed me to use Harper's technological support for this project. Very importantly, thank you to the Creative Homeowner family—my editor, Kathie Robitz, who is a very supportive person and an excellent editor. Also thanks to Tom Kalgren who helped get the ball rolling.

# Contents

**RIGHT** Because a fireplace is an architectural feature, its mantel and surround play an important role in establishing the decorative style in a particular room.

Are you thinking about installing a fireplace, updating an old one, or perhaps even adding a second or third one to your home? There is something beguiling about a fire that makes this amenity one of the most poular features in a home. A good-looking, efficient unit will increase the value of your home, not to mention your enjoyment of it. Thanks to smart new technology you have a choice between a traditional wood-burning model and a gas- or electric-powered unit. Or perhaps you're attracted to the charm of a stove. If you're not sure about what type of hearth appliance suits your needs, *Design Ideas for*

# Introduction

*Fireplaces* can help you to understand the differences between them. You'll find all the information you need to make a smart choice. You'll also see how other homeowners have made the most of their fireplaces all around the house and outdoors on patios, porches, and decks. *Design Ideas for Fireplaces* provides important facts about maintenance and safety, too, so that you can enjoy your appliance worry-free. Take a careful look at the following pages. Then let the fire lure you.

**ABOVE** White paint and a new mantel shelf with decorative brackets changed the look of this fireplace.

**LEFT** The formal fireplace is clearly the focal point in this room and anchors the furniture.

**OPPOSITE** A gas fireplace offers design flexibility. It's also convenient because it's easy to start and doesn't create a mess.

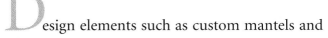

Design elements such as custom mantels and surrounds can enhance an architectural feature that has great appeal by its very nature. In addition, functional accessories—glass doors, screens, tool sets, andirons, and ash buckets—are available to blend with any decor: period, traditional, and high-tech modern designs. You can find them in an array of metal finishes, including wrought iron, brass, copper, pewter, and chrome. This chapter presents a variety of design ideas, but it starts with some practical tips to ensure the safest and most efficient use of your fireplace.

# Design Considerations

▌ **fireplace performance**

▌ **functional options**

▌ **woodstoves**

Andirons safely contain logs within the fireplace. The heirloom-quality brass set shown here is both beautiful and durable enough to last for generations

Even the most beautiful fireplace quickly loses its appeal if it doesn't work properly. That's why functional design elements have to be addressed before the aesthetic details are considered. In new fireplace installations, establishing the right location in the house is of primary importance. Many problems with a poorly drawing fireplace are a direct result of a less-than-ideal location. If you plan to install a new fireplace, you would be wise to locate it on an interior wall. Drafty, hard-to-start fireplaces are typical of fireplaces that have been installed on an exterior wall.

The chimney's location is also crucial to prevent wind-induced downdrafts and smoky fires. An otherwise cozy evening can become an unpleasant—and unhealthy—experience if you have to race around the room opening windows and doors and turning on exhaust fans to clear smoke billowing into the room from the firebox. A chimney should terminate through or near the highest roof in the house.

# fireplace performance

In addition, make sure that there is adequate air available to support proper combustion in the fireplace. If your house is new or has been recently remodeled, chances are it's airtight. If so, it's a good idea to consider a fireplace system that integrates outside air.

On the following pages you'll find other tips about improving fireplace performance.

**LEFT** This large 200-year-old fireplace was originally used for cooking.

**OPPOSITE TOP** The frame of these bifold glass doors reduces the size of the opening, balancing the fireplace-to-flue ratio.

**OPPOSITE BOTTOM LEFT** This electric fireplace does not require venting.

**OPPOSITE BOTTOM RIGHT** When fireplaces are on an exterior wall, patience and time-tested techniques can help overcome the fire-starting challenges and cold and draft issues.

# details make the difference

**OPPOSITE** A traditional design is always popular. If the fireplace is older, however, check for soot smudges in the opening. This suggests problems with downdraft and smoky fires.

**TOP LEFT** A fireplace in the master bedroom is a luxury that many of today's homeowners desire. However, make sure your choice meets building-code requirements for a bedroom installation.

**TOP RIGHT** A strong fire promotes warmer and more buoyant flue gases, and this standing fireplace screen provides spark protection.

**RIGHT** A fireplace on an exterior wall is more likely to smoke, as evidenced by the slight smoke stains that appear above the opening of this handsome Arts and Crafts design.

**LEFT** A brass-framed screen creates a picture-perfect effect with the fire as the subject of the composition.

**BELOW** Excellent draft is required to prevent smoke problems, which should be a consideration if you plan to place art on the mantel or on the wall above the fireplace. A chimney-top fan would increase the draft and reduce staining to the mantel and surround.

**OPPOSITE TOP** In a period home, this large walk-in fireplace opening was downsized by adding a custom metal fireplace hood and restraining grate system.

**OPPOSITE BOTTOM** A large fireplace, such as the one shown here, requires large volumes of air for combustion. The lack of sufficient combustion air can cause the fireplace to emit smoke into the room, sometimes after only an hour or two.

# enjoy a good burn

## sustaining a fire

- **Older homes** usually have combined air leaks measuring 36 in. in diameter as compared with those of new or remodeled homes with air leaks measuring just 8 in. in diameter. Essentially airtight, these energy-efficient homes may not provide enough air for combustion. The result is a poor fire that smokes.
- **An outside-air kit,** which provides the necessary amount of air to sustain a fire and prevent smoking, may be the answer.
- **A direct-vent gas fireplace** is another option for airtight homes. Direct-vent appliances are engineered to function independently, drawing air from outside the house.

**ABOVE** This fireplace looks as if it's been here for a century—but it's really a recently installed gas appliance. Realistic flames appear to be burning off the logs. Gas fireplaces may have a natural draft set, which relies on the proper combustion-air mix drawn from the room. Another type, a direct-vent gas unit, relies on outside combustion-air, drawn from the gap in between the inner and outer wall of the vent pipe.

**RIGHT** A direct-vent gas fireplace is a good option if the draft is sluggish. But if a wood-burning fireplace is a must-have, methods exist to introduce outside combustion-air to enhance draft. Chimney-top fans can provide additional help.

**ABOVE** Chimneys and fireplaces built into an interior wall of a house, as shown here, are more energy efficient and work better than those built on an exterior wall.

**LEFT** This fireplace features a combination of materials, textures, and colors in its design. The smooth, light-gray stone provides a facing for the fireplace and also for sidewalls of the alcove. The mantel shelf, with curves and scrollwork, holds objects that complement the tile pattern above it. The recessed spotlights highlight all of the handsome details.

# regarding draft and flow

▌ **Remember that warm air** rises and cold air falls. That's why a fireplace and flue on an exterior wall allow cold air to flow back into the room. The flue will probably need to be pre-warmed before starting the fire.

▌ **The traditional way to rewarm the flue** is to tightly roll a section of newspaper and light one end, holding it near the open damper (make sure to wear fireproof gloves). Another method is to use a hairdryer to warm the flue.

▌ **The flue should be a minimum** of one-tenth the size of the fireplace opening for proper draft. Under some circumstances, the flue may measure one-twelfth the the size of the fireplace opening. An experienced professional will be able to make an accurate assessment of the right flue size.

**LEFT**  This classic fireplace is on an exterior wall and may be affected by wind-related smoking problems.

**BELOW**  Large fireplaces installed in smaller rooms may not get sufficient combustion-air to sustain a fire. This problem can often be resolved by opening a window slightly.

**OPPOSITE TOP**  A gas starter pipe helps to ignite wood in a wood-burning fireplace.

**OPPOSITE BOTTOM**  The fire is delightful, but cleaning up could be a hassle. An ash vacuum cleaner can make the task easier.

A traditional wood-burning model—regardless of its drawbacks—is still a favorite of many homeowners. Familiar accessories that make a wood-burning fireplace safer and easier to use include andirons (or log retainers), glass doors, fire screens, heavy-duty grates, and ash containers that have a tight-fitting lid. But there are others.

Two of the more labor-intensive and time-consuming tasks—hauling wood and cleaning ashes—can be completely eliminated by using gas logs. However, if you're not willing to give up the characteristic look and aroma of real wood logs, products are available to make the hauling and cleaning tasks less arduous. For example, a sturdy wheeled cart specially designed for transporting logs makes filling the hearthside holder less of a burden.

For managing messy ash, an ash vacuum cleaner will help you do the job quicker and cleaner, and keep much of the dust and soot out of the air (and your breathing passages) and off your furniture and flooring. Fireplace owners who prefer a quick start over the patient process of kindling a flame may want to install a gas starter pipe, which can quickly and reliably ignite the logs.

If more heat and efficiency are primary concerns, consider a gas- or wood-burning insert that fits into an existing fireplace opening. With an insert, the hearth and mantel remain intact, with no modifications needed. In addition to providing heat, many of these units have large viewing windows, so much of the traditional ambiance is retained.

# functional options

## tradition versus today

# **h**olding the **h**eat

Glass fireplace doors are available in many sizes, styles, and for most applications (including corner and island models). Glass doors allow a view of the fire while keeping expensive heated air from escaping up the flue.

**ABOVE** Here's a fine example of an old country fireplace. Note the fireplace crane and a cast-iron spider, which were commonplace cooking implements until the advent of wood cookstoves. The large skillet with legs was designed to be placed directly on the bed of hot coals.

**OPPOSITE** This sleek, modern island fireplace is vented with a factory-built chimney. The screen should be closed to keep sparks from traveling onto and past the hearth. The large grate holds logs in place.

**tools and accessories enhance the experience**

**LEFT** When a fireplace is not in use, the firebox can look like a large black hole. In this case, the mantel and surround are decorative, but a good-looking screen would add to the fireplace's overall appearance.

**TOP LEFT** A grille at the top of the glass doors helps direct heat from the fire into the room.

**TOP RIGHT** The fireplace-to-flue ratio must be balanced. Some fireplaces, such as this one, are tall; the metal shield balances the ratio by lowering the fireplace opening.

**RIGHT** The rugged tool set shown with this fireplace blends well with the room's eclectic look. The traditional ball-top andirons combine attractive design and functionality.

# gaining heat from your fireplace

A typical masonry fireplace yields only about 10 percent of the heat value of the wood. In addition, if proper measures aren't taken, heated room air can be lost up the flue, actually costing more money than what might otherwise be saved by heating with wood. If heat is more important to you than open-hearthed ambiance, consider a wood- or gas-burning insert. The efficiency of these units is in the range of about 65–75 percent. A vent-free gas log set can increase efficiency to between 97–99 percent. However, vent-free log sets and heaters are not appropriate for every residential application. Before buying one of these appliances, get advice from a fireplace specialist.

**ABOVE** Here, the mantel is set as a stage for seasonal decorations. The hearth can also serve as a safe, indoor display area for candles—whether they're tea lights in carved pumpkins or candelabras with scented, smokeless candles. Candlelight provides an ambiance reminiscent of the warm fires of winter, no matter what's happening outside.

**RIGHT** Carefully selected functional accessories won't detract from a decorating theme. Here, the choice of a hanging spark screen ensures that the custom tiles framing the opening will be fully visible. Note the tool set, which complements the tiles and the mantel-shelf collection.

**LEFT** This fireplace features a large grate; andirons anchor the grate and limit the movement of the logs as they burn. Without such safeguards, burning logs could roll out of the fireplace and into into the room. A fireplace spark screen should be used to protect the wooden floor, preventing charring from popping embers.

**ABOVE** A corner fireplace is an interesting way to divide room areas while providing a wide-angle view of the fire. Spark screens and fireplace doors are widely available and are often included with a factory-built unit.

# **m**agnificent **m**etal **f**inishes

- **Hammered copper** harks back to Colonial days, when many fireplace tools and containers were crafted by master coppersmiths. However, hammered copper also fits well in Craftsman-style homes.
- **Solid brass** is often associated with traditional and period styles. Accessories made of this durable, rich-looking metal are enduringly popular, adding a stately presence in any decor.
- **Wrought iron** conjures up images of rustic Colonial fireplaces for which most tools were hand-forged by the local blacksmith. Wrought-iron accessories are unique in design, texture, and shape.
- **Chrome, stainless steel, pewter, and nickel** imply upscale, urban decor with an emphasis on a sleek, modern sensibility. Any of these—especially in a brushed finish—is the way to go if you want to give your fireplace an up-to-date appearance.
- **Antiqued bronze** is another option. It goes especially well with Old World or traditional interiors.

Wood-burning stoves are designed and engineered to be used as heating units. As a result, when it comes to operation for maximum efficiency and safety, the margin for error is slim. Two common mistakes people make are overloading a stove and damping it down to achieve long burn times; although the wood will burn longer, excess creosote buildup is the consequence. Under- or over-sizing the flue can also contribute to creosote buildup and cause draft problems.

# woodstove performance

**TOP LEFT**  Some fireplaces are designed to be heater-rated and can put out as much heat as a woodstove.

**TOP RIGHT**  A wood-burning stove installation such as this one illustrates the best-case scenario for venting: the stove pipe exits near the highest part of the roof.

**LEFT**  Older models burn inefficiently and have stricter installation clearance requirements. Some of these vintage units are best used as decorative accents only.

**RIGHT**  The tight installation of this stove is possible because most of the clearances are built into the unit. This stove provide heat and has the added feature of a bake oven above the firebox.

# time-honored charm

**OPPOSITE** This kiva fireplace is typical of the southwestern part of the United States. Some units can provide as much heat as a small woodstove.

**TOP LEFT** This older-model wood-burning stove is designed to operate with the doors fully open. The grayish-white discoloration of the stovepipe is an indicator of overheating.

**TOP RIGHT** A soapstone stove is used for both cooking and heating. Soapstone is a heat sink, which means it retains warmth long after the fire has burned out. Many of these units have built-in clearances.

**RIGHT** This antique stove is venting into the chimney above an unused fireplace opening. For this installation, a non-combustible, air-tight seal must be created in the opening to prevent smoke from entering the room.

**wood-burning stoves should be safe and efficient**

OPPOSITE  This stovepipe enters directly into the combustible wall with no wall protection, which can be dangerous.

ABOVE LEFT  A masonry heater retains a lot of heat yet burns very little wood. With most masonry heater units, a couple of fires during the day can make the house toasty from morning through the night.

ABOVE RIGHT  Unlike the logs shown here, seasoned wood, which produces more heat and less smoke, has checkmark lines radiating outward from the center.

RIGHT  A small woodstove heater provides enough heat to make this porch usable almost year-round.

# **c**ertified **w**ood-burning **s**toves

The United States Environmental Protection Agency (EPA) created a standard for wood-burning stoves as a result of the Clean Air Act. The New Source Performance Standard, implemented in 1990, sets limits for particulate emissions (soot, dust, and smoke). Measured in grams per hour, the current EPA-allowable particulate limit is 4.1 for a catalytic stove and 7.5 for a non-catalytic stove. A catalytic stove contains a honeycomb combustor, which must be cleaned regularly and replaced about every five years (more or less, depending on usage). A non-catalytic stove is engineered with a baffle, which isn't as efficient as a combustor but rarely needs replacing.

## today's models are ambient and efficient

**ABOVE** This vintage box stove provides a charming accent to the dining room. For the stove to burn wood safely, greater clearances from combustible surfaces and hearth protection are mandatory.

**OPPOSITE** With an ideal draft configuration, this wood-burning stove's pipe is straight and tall. Also note the stovepipe thermometer, which allows the user to gauge the needs of the fire.

## stove mechanics

Wood-burning stoves operate on the principle of supply and demand, and balance is the key to efficient functioning. The venting system is responsible for the "pull" that draws air in through the stove and up the flue. If the air entering the stove is restricted by damping down, the airflow and draft rates change, and creosote buildup accelerates. Flue sizing is also important—a flue that's too large or too small also throws off the balance.

### bright idea
### thermometer

Small, hot fires are most efficient, burn cleaner, and are safer in the long run than long, slow, burns. The only way to monitor a stove's operation is with a flue thermometer. The unit's manufacturer will suggest an optimal temperature range for your stove.

## 2

A touch of modern romance and extra warmth are just two reasons to consider installing a fireplace or woodstove if you are building or remodeling a house. Convenience and energy efficiency are two more, especially when you take into account the latest fireplace technology. Besides a traditional custom-built masonry fireplace, there are factory-built models, as well as gas- and electric-powered units that light or turn on at the push of a button. You can even regulate the flame height and the heat output on many of them. Turn the page for a rundown on more of today's options.

# What's New?

- masonry fireplaces
- exterior chimney designs
- factory-built fireplaces
- certified woodstoves
- gas fireplaces
- exterior fireplaces

Modern fireplaces incorporate many attractive features. Varieties and textures of brick and stone are among the finishing options that are available.

A traditional masonry fireplace is constructed of brick and mortar. New constructions and reconstructions often include either a metal or ceramic firebox. This type of firebox has double walls. Although a metal firebox is more efficient than an all-masonry one, it cools quickly after a fire goes out. Also, metal breaks down over time, a process that is called burnout. On the other hand, a ceramic firebox retains heat and continues to radiate warmth into a room even many hours after a fire has died. A ceramic firebox is more expensive than a metal one, but it is not subject to burnout.

# masonry fireplaces

**ABOVE LEFT** This masonry fireplace incorporates many features in its design, including a handsome stone surround and overmantel and built-in storage for wood.

**ABOVE** Gorgeous blue stone frames the firebox in this stately traditional masonry fireplace.

**LEFT** This newly built masonry fireplace burns cleanly and efficiently thanks to improved technology.

**RIGHT** A masonry fireplace may be constructed of bricks and mortar, but it can be finished in one of many ways. This one has been completed with local river rock to suit its location on the porch of a rustic vacation cabin.

# masonry materials

- **Brick** is a versatile building material that is available in a variety of finishes and colors. Reds, browns, blacks, white, speckled, textured, Old World, and American styles prevail. Brick can be stacked or used to create patterns such as basket weave or herringbone.
- **Ceramic tiles** can be used to frame the fireplace opening, creating a unique work of art. Tiles are widely available and come in many colors and styles. Some may be painted or feature a raised relief.
- **Stone** is a sturdy material that lends an air of permanence. Whether it's round field stones or custom-cut granite, marble, or slate, it's hard to beat the texture and strength that stone brings to contemporary fireplaces.

## focus on warmth

**ABOVE** This stone facade creates an earthy focal point in a room.

**LEFT** Sometimes brick is removed from old buildings, cleaned, and reused to create an authentic look in a period room, such as this one that depicts an old keeping room.

**OPPOSITE TOP** A heavy wooden beam serves as a mantel and adds character to this all-masonry fireplace.

**OPPOSITE BOTTOM** Even a traditional masonry fireplace can look modern on the outside. This one features a simple arched opening and no mantel.

### bright idea
## fresh look

You can paint a brick fireplace. At least one manufacturer makes a latex paint that is for this use. The formulation has extra adhesion to stand up to a fireplace's heat retention.

The chimney is an important part of your fireplace system—it makes a draft and flows air upward. As seen from the exterior, it contributes to the overall design of your house. With multiple available materials, styles, colors, and textures from which to choose, you can have a custom chimney with a dash of artistry and originality. Combine brick and stone for a blend of texture and color. Mortar dyes can be added to the mortar joints to outline or blend with bricks. New stucco is more elastic than its old version, so it's now okay for finishing chimneys that expand and contract slightly.

# exterior chimney designs

Create a pattern with brick or stone. This is always a way to make a chimney look outstanding. Step out the brick to form a corbel, providing a rim on the chimney top. Add accessories; a custom chimney top looks handsome above a hip-and-ridge roof. Install a clay chimney pot to emulate an Old World look. Or top the chimney with a European copper chimney pot, especially if there are copper gutters on your house. Take a look at the examples on these pages and see what might coordinate with your home's design.

**BOTTOM LEFT** Brick is always an attractive option for finishing a chimney. Here it coordinates with the style and color of the house.

**BOTTOM RIGHT** Maintain your chimney's exterior. Here, moisture damage on the top rows of brick should be repaired, then a breathable water-repellent sealer should be applied.

**RIGHT** This chimney has a little growing up to do. It should be taller than the roof to comply with fire codes and avoid wind-related downdrafts.

**OPPOSITE BOTTOM LEFT** This new chimney is protected by chimney caps and attractive new flashing—a wise investment.

**OPPOSITE BOTTOM RIGHT** A black chimney cap helps to keep rain and snow from entering the chimney, which otherwise acts as a large rain gauge. Moisture retention deteriorates the brick and mortar.

chimneys can add style

**OPPOSITE** The rugged stone texture on this chimney implies strength. The color combination complements the architecture of the house.

**TOP LEFT** A large chimney is an imposing element on the exterior of this house, so it's important to maintain the appearance of the brick.

**TOP RIGHT** A chimney in an older home can be made more energy efficient by using a top-sealing damper. It keeps cold air from entering and prevents heated air from escaping.

**RIGHT** A stone chimney is the perfect accent for this charming, English-style seaside cottage.

# **s**ensational **e**nergy **s**avers

Imagine opening a window and letting the heated or air-conditioned air escape to the outside. This scenario is very real when a fireplace is either missing the damper or the damper plate is warped or damaged. Conventional metal fireplace dampers, made of cast iron or steel, only provide a metal-to-metal seal at best. A money-saving strategy is to install a top-sealing fireplace damper, which has injected silicone or a silicone seal. This seal creates an air-tight, smooth closure, locking in heated or cooled room air. These dampers, which are made of cast aluminum or stainless steel, are rust and corrosion resistant. Because they are installed at the top of the chimney, they prevent entry of rain, snow, debris, and animals. They also provide a buffer to outside noise and are often used in noise-abatement areas close to airports.

Twenty years ago, the hearth industry rolled up its sleeves and started to refine engineering technologies, creating some of the highest-performing fireplaces available. Traditional wood-burning fireplaces have now moved to a new level, providing more heat and efficiency. Some of these devices are certified by the Environmental Protection Agency (EPA). Convenient gas-fired units offer options that include remote controls, thermostats, and more. Either type is a good investment and will increase the value of your home. Factory-built fireplaces are economical and quick to install. Industry standards are high, so if you follow the manufacturer's instructions, you should have an optimum system.

# factory-built fireplaces

**LEFT** Today's factory-built fireplaces feature many contemporary options, including artful finishing options.

**OPPOSITE TOP** Sleek, contemporary factory-built fireplaces are more economical than traditional fireplaces without sacrificing ambiance.

**OPPOSITE BOTTOM LEFT** Factory-built fireplaces are designed to circulate heat into the room through grilles in the frame.

**OPPOSITE BOTTOM RIGHT** New factory-built fireplaces can take diiferent shapes and sizes, creating the most unique feature in any room.

IIIIIIIIII **a factory-built unit allows for creativity** IIIIIIIIIII

## choices abound

A new factory-built fire-place can take many forms. Some are single-sided wood-burning units. Others may be three-sided peninsula units. Some are see-through with an opening in two adjacent rooms, such as the living and dining rooms.

ABOVE A factory-built unit can include options such as shelves, seating, unique mantels, and a choice of finishing materials, texture, and color.

OPPOSITE Unique materials can be used when constructing the facing. Also, because factory-built units have clearances built into them, they can be installed almost anywhere.

**LEFT** New woodstoves are engineered to provide heat performance and efficiency. Some units offer options such as a bake oven.

**BELOW** Relax and grab a book while this new contemporary-style stove sends out continuous warmth.

**OPPOSITE TOP** An EPA-efficient stove doesn't need to have contemporary lines and style. Vintage styles are popular, too.

**OPPOSITE BOTTOM** There are a variety of new paints available to make the stovepipe match the stove.

The Clean Air Act, enacted in 1990 by the EPA, demanded a refined wood-burning technology. Wood-stoves once emitted 30–50 grams of particulate (pollution) per hour. Now that they have been reengineered, they emit only 2–7 grams of particulate per hour. Efficiencies have increased from 40–60 percent to 60–80 percent. That means less smoke and ash and more heat output and fuel conservation.

Two new types of stoves have evolved from recent testing and engineering—catalytic and non-catalytic stoves.

*Catalytic stoves* burn more efficiently at 2–4.1 grams per hour. The feature responsible for this efficiency is a honeycomb ceramic catalytic combustor that's coated with noble metals. These metals ignite unburned flue gases when the catalytic unit is engaged—around 550 degrees. The catalytic unit requires periodic maintenance and replacement approximately every five years.

*Non-catalytic stoves* employ a baffle along the top of the firebox where air inlets aid the fire for a cleaner more complete burn. Also, insulated fireboxes help to raise the temperature for a more efficient burn. Non-catalytic stoves emit up to 7.5 grams per hour. Every stove sold today has a tag with the EPA-certification information including grams per hour and efficiency. These stoves have been tested to the New Source Performance Standard for Residential Wood Heaters.

# EPA-certified woodstoves

Gas fireplaces invite ambiance, convenience, and ease of use with the push of a button or flip of a switch. A little chilly? Set the thermostat so it kicks on at 70 degrees. Want to warm up the room quickly? Set the timer so that the fireplace runs for thirty minutes. Tired after a long day? Sit back and grab the remote. No, not the TV remote, the one that controls the gas logs. Curl up and relax watching the glowing logs, ember beds, and the flickering flame.

# gas fireplaces

**TOP LEFT** Because gas fireplaces don't require a large amount of space they can fit into almost any room, still providing ambiance and entertainment.

**TOP RIGHT** Most of today's gas-fueled fireplaces look just like wood-burning units.

**LEFT** Modern gas fireplaces feature realistic yellow flames and glowing embers, but they require little maintenance.

**OPPOSITE** A new gas log set can be installed in a conventional masonry fireplace, providing convenience and ease of use. If you wish, you can convert back to wood burning later.

# ambiance—the easy way

OPPOSITE A gas fireplace brings warmth into this ultra-modern kitchen.

ABOVE Gas units can be designed to coordinate easily with most interior-design styles.

ABOVE RIGHT Gas log sets usually include a burn media kit consisting of glowing embers, ash-like material, and cinders to simulate an original fireplace.

RIGHT Vent-free gas log sets are engineered to burn cleanly and efficiently, producing a minimal amount of soot.

Outdoor living rooms are a great investment, contributing to the appraised property value of your home. People are making more healthful choices, moving outdoors, enjoying the fresh air, and relaxing with family and friends. An outdoor fireplace that can be constructed of masonry or factory-built is a great addition. A masonry unit may be a full-size, custom-designed fireplace with a grill and a wood storage area off to the side. Or, it could be as simple as a campfire ring and fire pit.

# exterior fireplaces

Factory-built units can be designed to burn wood or gas. They may be elaborate, such as a see-through gas fireplace. This type can be installed on an exterior wall that is adjcent to a patio. A glass door allows you to enjoy the fire from both sides.

Many factory-built fireplace manufacturers provide modular units with grills that can be integrated into the design. To complete your outdoor living room, consider adding a wet bar, burners, refrigeration, storage cabinets—even a TV. Some modular designs are available online.

**LEFT** The new living room is situated outdoors. A fireplace and comfortable patio furniture provide many opportunities for relaxing outdoors.

**OPPOSITE TOP** A new outdoor fireplace can add value to the home while providing a new healthy environment for entertaining.

**OPPOSITE BOTTOM LEFT** This new masonry fireplace is made from stone cut in many shapes and sizes to enhance the facade.

**OPPOSITE BOTTOM RIGHT** Painted murals on the facade of this fireplace offer a unique one-of-a kind look.

**ABOVE** The smoke stains above the opening of this new fireplace are likely the result of leaves and trees blocking the flue outlet. The foliage should be removed because it creates a fire hazard.

**RIGHT** Not all outdoor fireplaces have to burn wood. Gas fireplaces, such as this one, provide an attractive option without the work of a wood-burning unit. Outdoor gas fireplaces are also designed with corrosion-resistant controls and components.

ABOVE This custom wood-burning design on a deck features a place for storing logs.

LEFT Today's outdoor fireplaces are constructed of a variety of materials from brick to metal. Chimney caps in all styles and sizes are available for outdoor fireplaces as well as for conventional units. These caps can help prevent traveling sparks from igniting nearby foliage or structures.

# outdoor living rooms

▌ **Outdoor living rooms** increase your usable space, costing less than a new addition. In most locations, an outdoor living area with a fireplace can be used seven to nine months out of the year.

▌ **Concrete patios and walkways** can be stamped, formed, and dyed to look like custom tile, flagstone, or brick, without the hefty price tag. Even molded and dyed pictures can be incorporated into your decor.

▌ **Local river rock** or cut stone recycled from an old building foundation gives the fireplace a unique outdoorsy feel with a piece of history attached.

▌ **Outdoor factory-built fireplaces** are constructed with stainless steel and other weather-resistant features for even extreme climates.

▌ **Economical chimineas or portable fire pits** are available to burn wood or gas. Be sure to use a listed fireproof pad if the unit is on a combustible surface, such as a wooden deck.

▌ **Many fireplace manufacturers** also manufacture grills and cooktops designed to be installed next to their factory-built fireplaces.

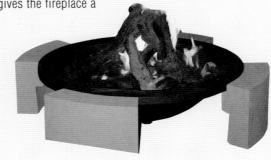

## 3

As long as the structure of your fireplace conforms to mandated building codes, style is your choice. You may want to stick with a look that is in keeping with the architecture of your house. Or if your house doesn't have a strong architectural point of view, you may want to strengthen it or change it by selecting a mantel and surround that clearly define a specific style. As with all design issues, personal taste is the ultimate determining factor. But if you're wondering where to begin, take a look at the many fireplace styles and finishing details on the following pages.

# Architectural Styles

▮ surrounds
▮ mantels

This fireplace's ornate, intricately carved mantel and surround feature numerous classical motifs that suit a grand interior.

The fireplace surround is an important architectural feature that can be a starting point for pulling together the interior design of the room. Fireplaces may be style-specific, such as Victorian, with its characteristic dark woods, marbles, and pictorial tiles. Or a style may be less clearly defined, in a category described generally as traditional, rustic, or contemporary. Explore the textures, colors, and ornamental features of various periods and styles and choose those that complement the style of your house or of the other design elements in your decor. A finished look might even incorporate elements from various architectural styles.

# surrounds

**TOP LEFT** Red brick has been a traditional favorite with fireplace lovers. Here, it showcases some heirloom pottery.

**TOP RIGHT** A massive limestone fireplace with a carved mantel is the focal point in this French-country-style great room. The look translates well to any Old World-inspired interior.

**LEFT** Cut stone has a refined rustic style. Here, the stone is a striking shade of blue. Wooden brackets support a reclaimed, rough-sawn wood beam that serves as a mantel.

**OPPOSITE** Wood paneling is the perfect surround for a fireplace in a period home, such as this Colonial. With built-in open and closed storage on either side, the fireplace wall becomes a major architectural feature.

# frame it in wood

## picture it

**A surround outlines** a fireplace much like a frame borders a picture. Classic finishing materials include: wood, brick, ceramic tile, river rock, and marble. Granite, limestone, and slate are popular today, but don't overlook trendy concrete and cast stone as more affordable alternatives.

**ABOVE** Because fine paneling can be expensive, consider using a more affordable type of wood, such as pine, that you can paint rather than stain. The red paneling here blends well with the brick, too.

**OPPOSITE** Taking a cue from the crown molding, the owners replicated the dentil molding and added an egg-and-dart motif to the mantelpiece of this Greek Revival-style fireplace. Topping the overmantel is an open-top pediment—another classical reference.

**define your style**

OPPOSITE Made of cast iron, this ornate surround is authentically Victorian. Today, you can shop for an antique or purchase a reproduction.

TOP LEFT Early Americana is an enduring style, and the stained-wood and red-brick surround, here, enhance its charm. However, the antique tinderbox is too close to the fire for safety.

TOP RIGHT A collection of vintage, hand-painted ceramic tiles adds personality to a standard fireplace opening.

RIGHT The honey color of the wood-paneled surround and overmantel brings warmth into this traditional-style living room. Marble tiles framing the opening coordinate beautifully with the wood's hue and add a sophisticated touch.

# a new aesthetic emerges

In the late 1800s, a renewed respect for hand craftsmanship and natural materials began to emerge in response to flamboyant Victorian decoration. The Arts and Crafts, or Craftsman, movement emphasized organic materials and forms—a plain surround and simple mantel, squared-off lines, and earthy colors are typical. The Art Nouveau movement (circa 1910-1918) followed. Fireplaces were decorated with sinuous organic motifs, particularly plant forms; ceramic tiles in pink, maroon, gray, and green were common. Fireplaces in the 1920s and 1930s assumed the features of the Art Deco movement: a new palette emerged, ranging from bright colors to soft pastels and inventive uses of inlays and lacquers.

**ABOVE** This elegant mantel and surround were inspired by an original Federal design. A curvaceous frieze panel separates the mantel from the opening.

**RIGHT** Stone tiles on the surround and hearth add a contemporary touch to a traditional design. A combination of moldings was used to create the mantel shelf, which was painted white.

ABOVE This period fireplace may have many tales to tell. Notice the surround, which is reclaimed brick. The unique, crafted firescreen featuring farm animals is whimsical. A mantel shelf was created using an old, hand-hewn beam.

LEFT More refined, this Georgian-style fireplace features side columns and moldings used to support the mantel shelf and decorate the frieze. The classic proportions of the individual elements give the fireplace elegant detailing.

# an array of finishing materials

▌ **Brick** comes in many colors and textures. It's a traditional choice that can suit both formal and informal designs.

▌ **Wood** is rich and warm, and it can be painted or stained.

▌ **Ceramic tile** has a European flair and gives you numerous options for adding color, pattern, a motif, or a mural.

▌ **Metal** surrounds are now available either commercially or on a custom-made basis. Sleek designs serve a modern sensibility. Vintage or reproduction **cast iron** evokes a Victorian look.

▌ **Stone**—granite, marble, limestone, and slate, in slab form or as tiles—are popular in contemporary homes of any style. Natural stone, such as river rocks—or their man-made counterparts—are well-suited to country or casual interiors.

▌ **Concrete** is affordable and creative. Today's sleek designs may feature color, texturous designs, or inlays.

**LEFT** A pink marble slip (or surround) brings color and elegance to this variation on a classic design, which features a fluted frieze panel below an understated mantel shelf.

**BELOW** A rustic fieldstone fireplace facade lends country charm here. A warm tone was chosen to stain the old wooden board that makes up the mantel. Combined, the stone and wood elements have an old-fashioned, warm and welcoming appeal.

**OPPOSITE TOP** A new fireplace can have the same appeal as a vintage model. Natural stone was used on this one to create the right informal feeling for a vacation house at the lake.

**OPPOSITE BOTTOM** A number of elements contribute to the eclectic style of this older model that has been refurbished over the years. To dress up the opening, Art Nouveau tiles have been installed above the opening. Some of the old bricks on either side of the opening have been painted to make them blend with the wall and form a decorative pattern.

## set the mood

# interest

▌ **Shapes** Many fireplaces are square or rectilinear, and the design effect can be boring. Masonry materials such as rounded and oblong field stone can be used to break up lines, adding interest.

▌ **Color** Bold colors make the fireplace a dominant architectural feature. Soft, subtle colors allow the fireplace to assume a background function when there's no fire. Consider the role of the fireplace in the context of your design scheme and choose colors accordingly.

▌ **Texture** Whether it's a smooth granite surround, rough and rugged brick, or polished marble, texture is a main contributing factor in creating the desired three-dimensional picture.

**bright idea**

## salvaged stone

Stone recycled from old foundations lends character and a sense of history to new fireplace exteriors and chimneys.

# ||||||||||||||||||| classic and contemporary |||||||||||||||||||

**OPPOSITE** A fireplace from the turn of the century looks stately with classical embellishments, such as moldings, columns, and the carved shell. Like the mantel and surround, the tiled frieze is original to the fireplace.

**TOP LEFT** Combining old and new, this direct-vent gas fireplace has an antique mantel and surround. The granite slip and hearth updates the look.

**TOP RIGHT** A polished black-granite surround framing the opening underscores the sleek minimalist look of this design.

**RIGHT** In another contemporary room, a neutral-color marble looks elegant. The polished-brass screen brings out the warm tones in the stone surround.

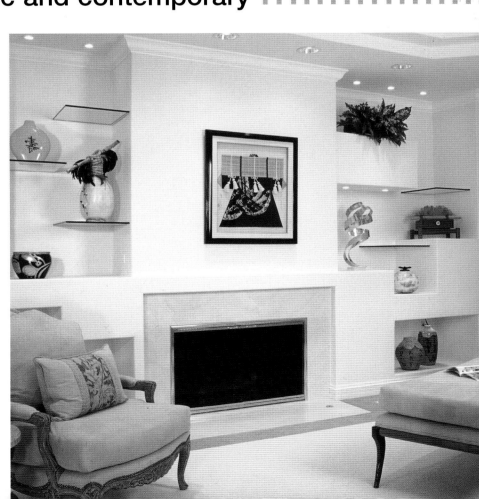

I n medieval times, the chimneypiece—a large, projecting hood—was built above a fireplace to direct the smoke up the chimney. Over time, fireplaces became smaller and the function of the chimneypiece diminished, gradually becoming a decorative shelf above the fireplace opening that is now most commonly referred to as a *mantel*.

Today the mantel serves as both an architectural element and as a focal point. This important design component may feature architectural reference points, such as moldings or brackets, that key into a particular style. Or it may be plain, allowing what's on the shelf—artwork or special accessories—to take all the attention.

# mantels

BOTTOM LEFT The severe simplicity of this rectilinear design is in dramtic contrast to the ornate antique mirror that hangs above the fireplace and and the mantel's eighteenth-century antique ormolu clock and garniture.

RIGHT A Victorian carved-marble fireplace with an arched mantel and a keystone is shown here in summertime when it's not in use. One way to camouflage the opening is with a plant.

BOTTOM RIGHT An English Rococo-style, this elaborate mantel and surround features side brackets and a shell-motif keystone.

OPPOSITE BOTTOM LEFT Intricate etching adds detail to this design carved from black marble.

OPPOSITE BOTTOM RIGHT A far simpler design, an American Federal-style fireplace in white-painted wood is elegant but understated.

look for fine craftsmanship

**LEFT** A carved limestone mantel rests on large, sturdy brackets. The design suits the scale of the room.

**TOP LEFT** Fluted pilasters with Ionic capitals and a carved frieze depicting urns and foliage dress up this design.

**TOP RIGHT** A similar design, in the English Regency style, has gracefully curved reeded pilasters with diagonal ribbons,

**RIGHT** A carved-wood mantel in the Geogian style pairs exquisitely with this surround that features brass and painted relief panels that depict classical decoration.

# **m**antel **a**ccents

Add personality to your fireplace by revealing your family's personalities on the mantel. Aside from photos, family memorabilia can include great-grandma's pince-nez reading glasses, an ancestor's favorite pipe, or a sampling from a present-day family member's collection of treasures, such as a few Waterford music-themed miniatures. Antique toys, such as small dolls or tin model cars add a whimsical touch, and an old copper weather vane with a verdigris patina can be a perfect complement to a country or rustic design scheme.

**LEFT** Magificent black marble with white veining makes this carved mantel and surround outstanding. It's definitely a look for a formal setting.

**BELOW** An ornate, Louis XV-inspired design has been carved from Carrera marble. Combined with a terra-cotta-tiled hearth and earthy art and accessories, the fireplace adds Old World splendor to this home.

**OPPOSITE TOP** The simplicity of this early eighteenth-century reproduction makes it versatile. The design would be at home in either a period, traditional, or contemporary interior.

**OPPOSITE BOTTOM** This modern picture-frame design is well-suited to a small space. It's fairly easy to build yourself, or hire a carpenter to make it.

## style allusions

## **c**urves

Circles and curves provide a graceful break to the typical fireplace's rectilinear and square shapes. Mantels are usually linear as well, but curved brackets can soften the lines and create visual interest.

A mantel could curve outward, arching away from the fireplace facing. Or, if the mantel shelf is brick, a brick or stone arch could be built above it.

A mantel supported by rounded logs has a down-home look. Add a cedar mantel slab with irregular rounded ends to enhance the rustic style.

IIIIIIIIIIIIIIIIIIIII **keeping the shelf simple** IIIIIIIIIIIIIIIIIIIIIII

# **c**ozy **d**esign

A humble but attractive brick fireplace has been refurbished with red paint here. Candle sconces on either side of the opening add an extra bit of ambiance. The simple mantel shelf is home to a collection of copper trinkets.

If your mantel is plain, dress it up with pottery, artwork, or a collection of family photographs.

**ABOVE** A minimum amount of accessorizing is perfect on this mantel shelf because the mirror above it is rather ornate.

**OPPOSITE** A small mantel shelf doesn't distract from the flat-screen TV that is built into the overmantel.

# make it personal

**OPPOSITE** For a cohesive look, match the molding you use on the fireplace surround and mantel to other trimwork in the room. Here, the crown molding was the inspiration for the style of the fireplace.

**TOP LEFT** Elaborate stenciling adds personality to this painted surround and mantel. Paint is an easy way to add custom touches.

**TOP RIGHT** A large framed print on the mantel leans against the wall. Displaying art in this way looks fresh and contemporary.

**RIGHT** A large paneled surround can be stained any color to suit your decor. This shallow mantel shelf leaves little space for display, so items have been arranged and installed on the wall above it.

**ABOVE** Consider replacing an old mantel and surround. That's what the homeowners did here, installing a handsome new oak surround and mantel. To make the fireplace blend with the pine paneling on the wall, they stained the two woods the same color.

**RIGHT** This dramatic arch sets off the fireplace wall in this room. The unusual mantel treatment was designed to bring the arch into scale with the fireplace opening. It was stained dark walnut to match the crown molding and the cabinets in the background.

ABOVE A shallow mantelshelf still has room here to display small figurines. Note the reeding and the Greek key motifs that have been carved into the wood.

LEFT Old pewter pieces enhance the authentic look of this small painted mantel. This shade of green was popular during Colonial times. Paint is a practical way to dress up inexpensive wood, such as pine.

# **a**mazing **m**antels

▌ **Wood** provides a variety of mantel options. Oak, walnut, bird's-eye maple, cherry, and mahogany all have a pattern and style uniquely their own.

▌ **Granite** offers an attraction of patterns and colors. Although a smooth material, granite gives the impression of textural influences in the ever-changing design in its surface.

▌ **Cut stone** offers texture, color and a personality with a history. Whether imported, or salvaged from a historical building foundation, there are many colors and varieties of stones available.

▌ **Man-made stone** is gaining popularity. It comes in a variety of faux stone looks and colors. Man-made stone is also more affordable than conventional stone.

▌ **Marble** is in a class of its own. It is associated with statues and building materials. Now it's widely available. Marble is attractive and holds it's own in the upscale building market.

OPPOSITE  A wild color scheme strikes a personality-plus note in this eclectic interior that combines modern lucite furniture with eighteenth-century antiques. Painting the Georgian fireplace was daring—to say the least!

TOP LEFT  A more traditional approach was maintained in this stately room. The surround and mantel have been painted white to match the woodwork, which stands out against cream-colored walls.

TOP RIGHT  Honey-tone wood frames the painted brick surround on this fireplace. The design would coordinate with almost any style interior.

RIGHT  A close-up view of this entablature shows that it is made up of various molding profiles, most notably dentil molding just under the cornice, or mantel shelf.

# **m**ajestic **m**antels

A handsome mantelpiece may deserve to stand on its own as an important architectural or decorative feature, but in most cases, accessories will add to its appeal. Framed art is a popular choice for mantel decor. However, size is important; a framed piece that is too small for the wall above the mantel will look insignificant over a fireplace. As a rule, the width of the frame should be two-thirds the width of the mantel. You may still hang a smaller piece if you pair it with another object to achieve the most attractive result provided that you consider overall scale and proportion. Also, think about how a piece—or grouping—of pottery may look in combination with the right piece of art.

**LEFT** A pretty carved-scroll detail gives this design extra flair without detracting from the mantel and surround's simple style. The black-marble slip looks elegant surrounded by the white panels.

**BELOW** Practically unadorned, except for the keystone and the recessed panel on the frieze and pilasters, this Federal-style mantel is as handsome as they come.

**OPPOSITE TOP** A paneled surround and tall overmantel add appropriate stature to the fireplace in this large room.

**OPPOSITE BOTTOM** The fireplace's deep-mahogany stain stands out against the medium-tone wood paneling here. Slate on the surround and hearth adds richness.

# details that draw attention

## **a**rt of **d**isplay

A grouping of objects on your mantel can be as simple or complex as you like. To make your display lively, choose a variety of shapes and sizes. For dramatic impact, group related objects that you can link in theme or color.

Remember that a symmetrical arrangement has classical overtones and will reinforce the formality of traditional designs. Stick with similar objects—a pair of Chinese jars or two matching candlesticks arranged in mirror fashion on either side of the shelf equidistant from the center. Or keep it simple with one important object in the center of the mantel.

Asymmetry brings a different, less formal dynamic to an arrangement. Try balancing one large object with several smaller ones on either side of the mantel.

**bright idea**

*shape it*

Can a rectangular mantel work with an arched fireplace opening? Imagine this: build the mantelshelf with brick and create a brick arch over the shelf to visually tie them all together.

ore than two centuries have passed since Benjamin Franklin designed the first American wood-burning stove in response to a shortage of firewood in Philadelphia. Today, firewood is in plentiful supply in most areas of the country, but necessity is still the mother of invention. Today's woodstoves are designed to burn more efficiently and much cleaner than earlier models. And with generous-size glass fronts on many new woodstoves, you still have the pleasure of watching a crackling good fire on a cool night.

# Wood-Burning Devices

- wood-burning basics
- maintenance
- types of wood
- buying wood
- starting a fire
- additives

A woodstove radiates it own special charm, with dancing flames, warmth, and designs to complement any decor.

**LEFT** The rolling flames, seen through the large glass window, are a result of the advanced engineering of today's woodstoves.

**BELOW** These bifold glass doors, folded or unfolded, allow a view of the flames.

**OPPOSITE TOP** For woodstoves, it's best to start with small pieces of wood, adding larger logs as the fire starts to "coal."

**OPPOSITE BOTTOM** A woodstove's capability as a heating unit makes the beauty of a crackling fire even more attractive.

A fundamental principle of safe, carefree indoor fireplaces is managing air flow. Before attempting to light a wood fire, make certain that the damper is open all the way. This allows a good draft (flow of air up the chimney) to prevent smoke from blowing back into the room. To ensure a good draft—particularly if your home is well insulated—open a window a bit when you are lighting a fire.

Also, build your fire slowly, which allows the chimney liner to heat. This will create a good draft, preventing downdraft, which occurs when cold air flows down the chimney and into the room. If the fireplace is properly maintained, the smoke shelf will redirect cold air up the chimney.

# wood-burning basics

**build a lasting fire**

**LEFT** As the fire burns, the logs may need rearranging or you may have to add new logs. A quality tool set is a necessity.

**ABOVE** A wood-burning system in a kitchen can be used for cooking as well as for aesthetics.

**TOP RIGHT** This attractive hand-forged standing screen is as important for safety as it is for looks.

**RIGHT** A fireplace truly completes the heart of the home, especially in an eat-in kitchen.

# **f**uel + **o**xygen + **h**eat = **f**ire

A fire that ignites easily and burns well and long without a lot of fussing is essential to the enjoyment of a wood-burning stove or fireplace. A few basics to remember include the following: first, get a small flame going with twigs, dark bark, or other kindling material, such as commercial "starter bricks" made from wood particles embedded in wax. Next, slowly add larger pieces of wood and logs as the flames build. Using well-seasoned, dry wood is essential; moisture prevents ignition. And of course, a fire won't burn without oxygen, so maintain air spaces between the logs. Encourage a quick start—or get a low-burning fire started again—by fanning the base with bellows.

Wood-burning fireplace and stove efficiency and safety is proportional to using the correct design for the space and the right burning techniques, in addtion to regular professional cleaning and maintenance. The venting system must be correctly sized to the device, and the device must be the appropriate size for the area that will be heated. Burning the right wood, maintaining the correct air-inlet adjustment, and keeping the flue and chimney clean makes fires burn efficiently. These measures also minimize the risk of a chimney fire from creosote buildup, reduce air-polluting emissions, and lessen firewood consumption.

# maintenance

**TOP LEFT** Some fireplaces are designed for heat output. Masonry releases heat long after the fire is extinguished.

**TOP RIGHT** For a roaring fire, open the damper wide and use seasoned, dry hardwoods. Keep the fire stoked, and don't encourage it to smolder.

**LEFT** To make a masonry fireplace system more energy-efficient, add a set of glass doors or a top-sealing damper.

**OPPOSITE** Manufactured units such as this kiva-style fireplace tend to be more efficient than traditional fireplaces. Factory-built units have to be listed and tested, so you know that the designs are engineered to meet stringent standards.

# ||||||||||||||||||||||| romancing the fire ||||||||||||||||||||||||

**OPPOSITE** A clean-burning fire is the reward for properly maintaining your fireplace system.

**ABOVE** Dining in front of a smoke-free, crackling fire on a cool day is a wonderful way to enjoy a meal.

**TOP RIGHT** Standard masonry fireplaces radiate heat into the room. This means objects facing the fire will tend to be warm on that surface, whereas the side of the object facing away from the fire will be cooler.

**RIGHT** A cast-iron fireback can be used to create a heat-sink, collecting heat and radiating it back into the room.

Burning the right type of wood makes the difference between an efficient, long-lasting, clean fire or one that's smoky and full of creosote. Hard, dense woods are ideal as fuel. (As a rule of thumb, hardwood comes from deciduous—leaf-shedding—trees such as oak, maple, walnut, birch, beech, and ash.) Because of their density, hardwoods burn longer and hotter. Avoid burning soft woods such as pine and fir because they tend to have a high content of creosote-building resin. Burn only wood that has been seasoned for at least six months. A good visual clue to proper seasoning is the appearance of small cracks radiating out from the center of the wood.

# types of wood

**LEFT** This fire will burn for hours because the hardwood logs are long lasting.

**OPPOSITE TOP** Small logs create a small, hot fire. Larger logs can be added later when the coals are sustained.

**OPPOSITE BOTTOM LEFT** Some highly efficient fireplace systems don't require a fireplace grate.

**OPPOSITE BOTTOM RIGHT** The warm glow of candles provides a pleasing alternative to a fire on warm evenings.

**LEFT** Make sure that the firewood has been seasoned for at least six months.

**BELOW** When you purchase wood, always check the maximum length of the logs to avoid having to cut them to size later.

**OPPOSITE TOP** This pile of split wood is ready whenever the homeowners need it.

**OPPOSITE BOTTOM** Firewood can be stored in baskets, racks, or creative containers such as this copper tub.

Any individual with a pickup truck, a chain saw, and access to a wooded area can set up shop as a seller of firewood. Unless the seller is recommended by someone you trust, becoming a smart firewood consumer can be an expensive learning curve. Know what you need and ask for it up front.

Wood is ordered by the cord (4 × 4 × 10 feet packed tightly, or a total of 128 cubic feet). When you talk to a vendor, first ask what type of wood is available. If the answer is anything other than hardwood, shop elsewhere. (See page 100.) Also, ask how long the wood has been seasoned. Wood should be seasoned for a minimum of six months.

Next, specify the maximum length you want your logs to be. Wood that's too long can be a big problem, particularly if you have a woodstove. Even an additional 2 inches makes a difference if you can't angle a log in order to close the stove door.

Lastly, if the price sounds right and you decide to purchase the wood, ask whether the vendor will stack it when he delivers it. If so, find out the charge for stacking—few vendors do this for free.

# buying and storing wood

**RIGHT** Firewood must be kept dry. If wet wood is put into a stove, the moisture would have to be driven out of the wood before it can start to burn. This lowers the flue gas temperature, causes more smoke emissions, and increases the potential for creosote buildup, higher maintenance costs, and a chimney fire.

**ABOVE** Wood should never be stored on top of or too close to a stove because it could cause a fire. This antique coal bucket is an attractive way to keep extra logs on hand safely.

**LEFT** This large, brick family-room hearth features a convenient built-in nook for storing extra logs a safe distance away from the fire but within handy reach.

# smart buying and storing tips

Wood that is stored out in the open on the ground can soak up a lot of moisture, decay, and harbor insects, such as termites and carpenter ants. Always store wood elevated off the ground so air can circulate under it.

Any number of natural and manufactured materials, and a little ingenuity, can result in a very serviceable, attractive home-built storage system. Two requirements: build it sturdy, and make sure it keeps firewood off the ground. The simplest, least expensive wood rack consists of a couple of recycled warehouse pallets placed on the ground between two trees. The wood is stacked perpendicular to the trees, which provide natural vertical side rails.

Commercial racks are available that can hold as much as a half-cord or even a cord of wood. Some also have optional zip covers to keep wood covered.

Veteran fire makers all have their own special tips for starting a fire, but there's an easy way to do it that works fine. After opening the damper, set the kindling. Place fatwood, a piece of wax-based fire-starter brick, or three or four sheets of tightly crumpled newspaper on the floor or grate. Then

# starting a fire

take a handful of small, dry pieces of wood, and place them on top in a crisscross pattern, leaving air space between the pieces. Hold a flame to the base, and then once it has ignited the materials, gradually add larger wood pieces. Finally, crisscross several logs on top.

**BOTTOM LEFT** For a robust blaze and a fire that's long lasting, you'll need hard, seasoned logs.

**BOTTOM RIGHT** A gas starter pipe can be installed in a masonry fireplace to start the fire quickly.

**RIGHT** This fireplace is a vision of warmth and beauty.

**OPPOSITE BOTTOM LEFT** Commercial fire starters make for quicker, easier starts than the traditional materials: matches and kindling.

**OPPOSITE BOTTOM RIGHT** It's best to start with small logs or split logs and add to the fire with larger logs later.

**LEFT** Another way to start a fire like this one is with a ceramic ball that has been saturated with a flammable liquid such as kerosene. Place it under the kindling, and light it.

**BELOW** Don't forget: when you add logs, place them in a crisscross pattern on top of the other kindling.

**OPPOSITE TOP** A fireplace that is hard to start may need draft assistance from a chimney fan.

**OPPOSITE BOTTOM** Arrange furniture to take advantage of your fireplace. In this room, there's a cozy arrangement of comfortable seating in front of the fire.

# a great blaze begins with the right wood

## light up

Up to half the weight of fresh-cut wood is water. Proper seasoning, which takes between 6 and 12 months after cutting, reduces the water content in wood to about 20 percent. Any water that remains in wood that's used in a fireplace or stove will boil off and, in the process, consume heat energy.

If you've purchased a supply of wood that hisses, sizzles, and is hard to ignite, store it in a dry place for a few more months. Always purchase seasoned wood, and then stack it properly—covered on top—to keep it dry.

**bright idea**

*it takes two*

To maintain a good fire, there should always be at least two logs, spaced about 1–3 inches apart. Turbulence (air movement) sweeps through the spaces, helping to dry and ignite the wood.

Chimneys should be professionally cleaned at least once a year, but in between, chemical chimney cleaners can help control creosote. Creosote is a black, tacky, crusty substance formed when the smoke and gas from burning wood condense on the lining of a chimney. Creosote buildup reduces the efficiency of a woodstove or fireplace and poses a potential fire hazard. Some creosote-removal products are available in powder, granule, or liquid form and should be sprinkled or sprayed on the fire. Another type is a chimney sweeping log, which contains chemical additives that are released as the log burns. In whatever form, creosote removers basically work by crystallizing creosote, making it brittle and allowing it to fall away from the chimney surface.

# additives

Flame enhancers are market-approved additives available as crystals or flame sticks. When tossed into a fire, they cause the flames to burn blue and green, turning an already entrancing show into a color spectacle. They should be used only on well-vented wood fires in fireplaces, firepits, chimineas, and woodstoves. Be cautious when using them at camp fires, and never use them over a cooking fire. These products contain toxic chemicals, so keep them away from children and pets.

**LEFT** A chemical catalyst helps reduce creosote buildup in this fireplace and makes cleaning it easier.

**OPPOSITE TOP** You can turn flames like these into a green and blue show by adding a commercial flame enhancer.

**OPPOSITE BOTTOM LEFT** A chemical creosote-removing catalyst can be sprayed inside this firebox after each use.

**OPPOSITE BOTTOM RIGHT** To keep this sleek new fireplace in good working order, the owners must adhere to yearly professional cleaning.

**careful what you burn**

**OPPOSITE** For a safe burn like this one, chemical creosote-reducing additives come in many forms: spray liquids, granules, and sticks that can be thrown into the firebox.

**ABOVE** Burning driftwood, cans, plastic, Christmas trees, or garbage in general, seems unimaginable in this beautiful fireplace.

**TOP RIGHT** The inside of a fireplace can deteriorate as a result of using improper additives.

**RIGHT** Liquid chemical products are widely available to remove smoke stains from the inside of a masonry firebox.

# **w**hat **n**ot to **b**urn

The only ingredients in a safe fire are a flame source; wood, paper, or commercially produced kindling; and dry, seasoned hardwoods. Never use gasoline or other flammable liquids to start or rekindle a fire. The only exception is the Cape Cod-style firestarter, which uses a ceramic ball soaked in kerosene. (See page 108 for additional information.) Flammable liquids vaporize and can travel the length of a room. When the vapors reach a flashpoint, they can explode—a dangerous situation.

Also, never burn chemically treated wood, driftwood, tin cans, or anything that is not specifically mentioned in your appliance's owner's manual.

## 5

Advances in technology have made gas fireplaces, stoves, and inserts increasingly popular, with about one million units sold every year. That's more than 60 percent of all hearth-appliance sales. Gas hearth products are also one of the leading optional features in a new home, and no wonder. In addition to the convenience, realism, and warmth these products offer, most gas units burn cleaner than even the most-efficient wood-burning stoves available. Options include push-button remote controls, thermostats, automatic timers, hand-painted ceramic or glowing fiber logs, and ember beds.

# Gas Fireplaces & Stoves

I **gas basics** I **location options**

I **fireplace types** I **direct-vent**

I **vent-free** I **natural vent**

This see-through gas fireplace, enclosed by glass doors, provides multi-room access to a cozy fire.

# gas basics

Gas hearth units are designed to burn one of two types of fuel: natural gas or propane. Both are fossil fuels and good sources of heat, but their chemical compositions are not the same, and they have a number of other different properties. Appliances are designed differently according to the type of fuel that powers them. (Some—definitely not all—appliances can be converted from one fuel type to the other.) Natural gas is lighter than air and, naturally, rises. On the other hand, propane is heavier than air and sinks. Therefore, the ignition and burning mechanisms for natural-gas and propane-fueled fireplaces must be located to accommodate this. Natural gas must be delivered to its location of use from a central source by a system of pipes, created and maintained in most cities and towns by your gas utility provider.

Propane (also commonly called liquefied petroleum, or LP gas) exists in a liquid form when it's contained in a pressurized tank. It vaporizes immediately when it's exposed to air. For this reason, propane is easily transportable. This makes the use of gas appliances possible when natural supply lines aren't available, such as in some rural regions of the country.

**BOTTOM LEFT** A gas-fueled stove provides great ambiance without a fuss.

**RIGHT** This gas log set features hand-painted ceramic logs. When the fire is out, the logs are still realistic.

**BOTTOM RIGHT** Although toolsets aren't needed for gas appliances, they make attractive accent pieces.

**OPPOSITE LEFT** Screens or glass doors can be used with a gas fireplace.

**OPPOSITE RIGHT** This distinctive arched opening showcases the realistic flames in this gas fireplace.

## enjoy a modern marvel

### easy does it

**Power outages** don't usually affect today's gas appliances. Most are equipped with a spark igniter or can be lit manually with a match or butane flame. Batteries in the hand-held unit and the remote control unit, which sits near the firebox, require periodic replacement.

ABOVE Although gas hearth products are the result of recent engineering advances, these appliances complement any style. This fireplace has a traditional design, with its carved mantel and standing firescreen. The gas burner is concealed within the ceramic log set.

OPPOSITE A dining room is a perfect location for a fireplace, especially a gas unit, because all it takes to get a fire started is the push of a button or flip of a switch.

**LEFT** Gas hearth appliances can be ignited by hand with the push of a button or flip of a switch.

**BELOW** This beautiful, realistic-looking gas log set is made of ceramic fibers. When the logs heat up, they glow, simulating burning wood logs. The burn media below the logs simulate ashes, enhancing the realism. The special grate, andirons, and fireback are complementary elements in this uniquely designed set.

**OPPOSITE TOP** With designs available for any room, gas fireplaces and stoves can provide zoned heating.

**OPPOSITE BOTTOM** Proper draw can be a problem with a traditional fireplace in a tightly insulated home. Direct-vent gas units are ideal for these settings: they pull air for combustion from outside the house and exhaust to the outside through the same vent system.

## gas units are versatile

# gas logs

- **Gas log sets** come with gas stoves, fireplaces, and inserts. Ceramic fiber, concrete, and refractory logs are available in a variety of styles and finishes that resemble wood species such as oak, birch, and hickory.
- **Gas logs** are also available to take the place of wood for existing wood-burning fireplaces. Vented logs should be used with the damper permanently fixed in the open position or removed entirely. Glass doors are a must to prevent heated or cooled air from escaping when the fireplace is not in use.
- **Unvented logs** can be used with the damper completely closed. They provide more heat but are less realistic than vented logs. With partially vented logs, the damper can be closed up to 90 percent.

Because of the venting options available on today's gas fireplaces and stoves, these units can be installed almost anywhere. For placement on an outside wall, the vent is run through the wall. Gas units that are located on interior walls or in islands and peninsulas can be vented through the ceiling to the roof. Otherwise, vents can be run into the ceiling and out through an exterior wall. This flexibility makes it possible to save energy dollars by providing (or supplementing) heat in rooms that are being used rather than running the central heating unit for the entire house.

# location options

**TOP LEFT**  A special catalytic spray is available to help eliminate soot on gas logs. Ask your installer for specifics.

**TOP RIGHT**  Gas logs can be installed in a traditional masonry fireplace. In this case, they won't provide any more heat than wood logs, but they offer the same ambience with greater convenience.

**LEFT**  This gas stove emulates a traditional wood-burning unit. The large arched viewing window provides a view of a realistic fire.

**OPPOSITE**  You can use a gas fireplace on an interior wall. This one features a reproduction of a Victorian style mantel and facade.

**LEFT** Direct-vent gas units can be vented through the wall, allowing installations in any area of the house.

**ABOVE** Gas stoves and fireplaces are a good source of supplemental heat and a great back-up heating system during power outages.

**TOP RIGHT** As with most masonry fireplaces, gas-fueled models can be used with almost any style mantel and hearth.

**RIGHT** The ceramic or refractory logs in gas log sets are created in molds made from real wood logs. The material may be cement, extruded-bisque ceramic clay, or ceramic fibers.

# **p**ortable **d**esign

**Gas fireplaces and stoves** eliminate the tiresome job of hauling and storing wood logs, the fussing with tools to keep a blaze going, and the messy ash cleanup. These attributes also make the use of gas fireplaces and stoves a reasonable space-heating option in locations such as bedrooms, where ash and spark control pose problems.

In a kitchen, a gas appliance allows the cook to enjoy the comfort of a fire while preparing food without the need to monitor the fire. Of course, a fireside dinner is always enjoyable, especially when all you have to do is push a button.

For rooms on an upper level of a house, there's no need to transport ash cans or wood up and down stairs.

**ABOVE** The most common cause of soot buildup when burning vented gas logs is improper arrangement. When flames touch the underside of the logs, impingement occurs and the combustion process stops. The incomplete burn results in the formation of black deposits. Check the owner's manual for log placement instructions.

**RIGHT** Some stoves generate as much as 28,000 Btus, which is more than enough to heat a large space. A wall-mounted thermostat lets you control the temperature.

**ABOVE** Grime accumulates over time on the artificial embers and ashes at the bottom of a gas log set. These elements can be replaced as needed.

**LEFT** Instant on-and-off flames is just one convenience of a gas fireplace. In addition, the flame height and look of the fire are adjustable, as is the heat output. The installation of gas logs in an existing masonry fireplace is not a do-it-yourself project; for proper and safe operation, use a certified professional installer.

# **t**he **g**rate **o**utdoors

The popularity of outdoor gas fireplaces is easy to understand because they offer the opportunity to extend the outdoor-living season.

Gas fireplaces provide great design flexibility. Choose a traditional style to simulate an indoor living room, or go high-tech. Unique see-through installations on exterior walls allow views of the patio or deck from inside the house. The two-way view visually expands the home by more fully incorporating the "outdoor room."

A round design is accessible from all sides and allows more people to enjoy the view and the warmth of the fire—a great advantage for homeowners who like to socialize.

Outdoor gas firepits are less expensive than fireplaces or stoves, but they don't compromise on ambiance. Most can be hooked up to a propane tank, such as the type used for barbecue grills.

## great design possibilities

**OPPOSITE** This attractive gas fireplace can be ignited with a simple flip of a switch or push of a button. No electricity is required unless a heat-circulating fan is installed.

**ABOVE** Gas logs complement the rugged good looks of this fireplace system. Glowing embers below the logs add a realistic touch.

**TOP RIGHT** The handsome sturdiness of this direct-vent gas stove perfectly suits the rustic look of the surrounding brick wall and floor.

**RIGHT** Don't assume that this exquisitely carved mantel frames a wood fire. Gas logs can burn on this hearth.

# fireplace types

There are three types of gas fireplaces (and stoves), classified according to how they vent: direct-vent, top vent design, and vent-free. With all three types, the products of combustion are vented outside the home using inexpensive, "class B" pipe that's similar to what's used on gas water heaters. *Direct-vent* units don't need a full chimney and can be vented directly through a wall or roof. They use two pipes—one to bring in combustion air, the other to remove the products of combustion. *Top-vent* designs are ideal for installation in an existing fireplace because they use a metal or brick chimney (not just a vent pipe) as the exhaust vent. Air for combustion is drawn from inside the house.

*Vent-free* appliances operate without exhaust vents. Before settling on a vent-free product, some investigation is in order. Ideally, they don't affect indoor air quality, but an oxygen depletion sensor (ODS) is incorporated on vent-free units. The ODS automatically shuts off the gas if oxygen levels drop too low. Also, even when oxygen is adequate, individuals with respiratory problems such as asthma may be sensitive to the slight odor associated with unvented gas, or they may experience discomfort from a small decrease in oxygen levels in the room. Finally, unvented gas appliances are prohibited in some states, so check the regulations in your area before shopping.

**LEFT** Because the surface of a gas stove is not confined within a wall, more usable heat is radiated into the room. Also, gas stoves come with a fan that circulates the heated air throughout the room.

**OPPOSITE TOP** This see-through fireplace design allows views of the fire from adjoining rooms.

**OPPOSITE BOTTOM LEFT** A contemporary facade frames these gas logs.

**OPPOSITE BOTTOM RIGHT** Heat from this model flows into the room through the grilles in the glass doors.

Direct-vent gas appliances have a unique design that permits locating one of these units anywhere in a house. Combustion air is drawn from outside and pulled through the space between the inner and outer walls of the vent pipe. The flue gases are expelled through the inner wall of the pipe. Direct-vent units—also known as "sealed combustion fireplaces"—have a sealed-glass front that should never be removed, except by a qualified technician for maintenance and trouble-shooting. Heat from direct-vent units radiates from the gas logs, glass front, and chamber walls.

# direct-vent

**TOP LEFT** With glass on three sides, this "open-view" fireplace is a handsome room divider.

**ABOVE** This corner-installed direct-vent fireplace incorporates a gas log set in a fine piece of furniture. Direct-vent systems allow horizontal venting, avoiding the costs of a chimney system.

**LEFT** Paneling distinguishes this model, which features a direct-vent gas log set with glowing fiber embers.

**OPPOSITE** See-through, direct-vent gas fireplaces generally function better than traditional see-through wood-burning fireplaces. A wood-burning fireplace requires a flue size equal to approximately one-tenth of the fireplace openings combined. Direct-vent units are engineered to function with a smaller vent.

Vent-free gas appliances are designed to burn efficiently and very cleanly—the combustion process burns virtually all of the gas. However, because these products essentially vent into the room, the room must be the right size for the model that you choose—room oxygen levels can be expected to drop slightly, even when the appliance is functioning perfectly.

As a safety measure, vent-free units are equipped with an oxygen depletion sensor (ODS) that shuts off the gas burner when oxygen falls below a set limit. If a vent-free appliance is not used for a long period, the ODS can sometimes become dusty and may shut off the gas despite adequate oxygen. If this happens, a gas technician can clean the unit to restore usability. In terms of aesthetics, there have been improvements.

# vent-free

Formerly, vent-free units provided only a blue flame that had about the same ambiance as a pilot light in the kitchen stove. Today's vent-free log sets burn with attractive, more-realistic yellow flames. The logs, made from molded refractory cement or ceramic material, glow when they have been heated, closely simulating a burning wood fire. The logs fit together like a puzzle, so they must be installed according to the diagram in the owner's manual. Improper placement can cause unsightly and messy soot to accumulate on the logs, requiring removal with special cleaners.

**BOTTOM LEFT** Vent-free gas logs fit together like the pieces of a puzzle.

**BOTTOM RIGHT** Gas fireplaces and stoves are designed to burn either natural gas or propane. This option allows homeowners without access to a gas pipeline to use gas-hearth appliances.

**RIGHT** Vent-free gas stoves provide an excellent return on your heating dollars.

**OPPOSITE BOTTOM LEFT** A gas fireplace is an effective source of supplemental heat, and it has a more realistic flame than vent-free appliances.

**OPPOSITE BOTTOM RIGHT** Vent-free gas logs incorporate an oxygen depletion sensor that can become blocked with dust, shutting off the system. Consult a gas technician for cleaning.

**LEFT** A vented gas appliance should never be located in a bathroom or bedroom unless it's listed for this use and installed according to the manufacturer's specifications.

**BELOW** Natural draft see-through fireplaces must be vented vertically. Most use a class-B gas vent, like the one used on gas furnaces.

**OPPOSITE TOP** Gas log sets that operate on natural draft must be used with the damper fully open.

**OPPOSITE BOTTOM** The flame in this stove provides heat that radiates through the protective glass.

Natural-vent fireplaces are gas units that vent by natural draft, as did most of the early gas fireplaces and space heaters. This means that the natural buoyancy of the flue gases carries the products of combustion up the flue. The draft also draws air for combustion into the fireplace, so some units require the glass doors to be open during use. Venting is usually done with a class-B gas vent, which has an inner wall of aluminum, an air space, and an outer wall of galvanized metal.

Natural-vent gas-burning units are available in several configurations: gas fireplaces, gas stoves, or gas logs that are installed in a traditional masonry fireplace. Natural-vent gas logs used in an existing fireplace must be operated with the damper in a fully open position. In fact, the building codes in some locations require that the fireplace damper be removed or permanently fixed in the open position. Many manufacturers provide a damper stop that keeps the damper open a minimum of 1 inch when the fireplace is not in use.

Options include a fan kit for convection heating, remote-control operation, an on-and-off wall switch, wall-mounted or remote thermostats, firebrick designs, and decorative faceplates.

# natural vent

## 6

Do you long for the cozy charm of a fireplace but for whatever reason think you can't have it? An electric fireplace is the answer. Forget what you know about them from the past. Today's models are realistic and handsome. They also come with desirable amenities, such as temperature-control heating systems and, in the case of at least one manufacturer, an air purifier. Other extras include a masonry firebox, variable-speed flame, and realistic logs. You'll find an array of finishing options, too, ranging from classic traditional wood cabinets to stone and metal. Here's what's in the stores.

# Electric Fireplaces

▌ the basics

▌ versatile and carefree

Electric fireplaces use little space. They don't require a chimney and can be built-in, as is this one, or installed in a free-standing cabinet.

Electric fireplaces and stoves are easy to use and install. These affordable, mostly portable devices are ideal for any room in the house and for an apartment or condominium. All you usually have to do is bring one home from the store and plug it into a standard 110/120-volt receptacle. Voilà, instant ambiance! There are no walls to knock down, no necessary venting, and no maintenance. However, some electric fireplaces must be hard wired, which means you may have to hire an electrician. Large models may require a 220-volt electric receptacle—the type needed to run a room air conditioner—depending on the requirements of the unit's heating system. If you don't have the proper

# the basics

receptacle in the room where you plan to use the fireplace, an electrician can take care of that for you, too. The controls for most electric fireplaces and stoves are located behind a panel on the front of the unit. Some models come with a remote control that lets you turn on the unit and adjust the heat output, fan speed, and simulated flame flicker from a comfortable seat, the bed, or even the bathtub. Also, keep in mind that an electric fireplace that provides heat is almost 100 percent efficient. Actual heat output varies between models, but the average 4,500 Btus—compared to a gas unit's 20,000 Btus—can warm a small room.

**LEFT** Although this stove looks like it's burning wood, it's actually simulating the real thing. Practical and easy-care, this electric unit is portable and doesn't require specific floor protection.

**OPPOSITE TOP** Some electric fireplaces, such as this metal-framed model, have a "glowing ember bed" for the most realistic look.

**OPPOSITE BOTTOM LEFT** This cabinet makes a handsome traditional statement.

**OPPOSITE BOTTOM RIGHT** Glass doors come with this model.

**LEFT** Designed to conserve space in a small room, this unit has been hard wired and recessed into the wall. A simple mantelshelf adds a touch of elegance.

**BELOW** This portable model in a pewter frame looks picture perfect and contemporary on an accent wall.

**OPPOSITE TOP** A prefabricated mantel and surround provide handsome housing for an electric fireplace on an interior wall.

**OPPOSITE BOTTOM** A stone mantel, surround, and hearth add a realistic look to this design.

Because electric fireplaces and stoves have so few requirements, they are perfect for homeowners or renters who want the look and charm without the hassle and expense of installing the real thing. You don't have to worry about clearances or approval from your local building department, either. These devices have already been tested and cleared for safety.

Moving? Take your electric fireplace or stove with you. The cabinets used with electric fireplaces usually don't weigh much more than standard entertainment centers, making them relatively easy to transport. Some disassembly or extra packing may be required to protect the logs and glass doors, but that's all.

If you have an old, inefficient fireplace, you might consider refurbishing it with an electric insert. However, you'll need a surround that fits around the insert; a gap between the firebox and the surround would spoil the realistic appearance—and hence the ambiance—of your appliance. You can buy a cabinet separately or have one custom made.

# versatile and carefree

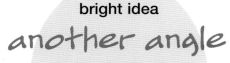

**bright idea**

*another angle*

Are you limited by space considerations? Consider an electric fireplace that's designed to fit snugly into a corner.

**ABOVE**  A homeowner upgraded the look of his electric unit with stone tile. Because an electric fireplace does not require a chimney, it is an economical choice for installation and maintenance reasons.

**RIGHT**  An elegant marble surround and a classic wood mantel and frieze realistically recreate the look of an authentic period wood-burning fireplace.

**ABOVE** House one of these devices this way, in a traditional wood surround, or in a contemporary frame made of metal that you can hang on the wall like artwork.

**LEFT** This model comes fully assembled—there are no special tools or trim kits that you need to finish it. Take it out of the box, plug it in, and turn on the power.

# **a**ttractive **o**ptions

▌ **Today's electric fireplaces and stoves** are more realistic and aesthetically pleasing than in the past. Simulated fires set the stage with faux logs, grates, and glass doors. Some models boast a "glowing ember bed."

▌ **An electric fireplace may feature** an additional, economical night light incorporated into the fireplace unit.

▌ **Adjustable flame speed** is an attractive option in electric fireplaces. Set the speed on high for the effect of a fast-burning fire. Decrease the flame speed to low, for a slow flickering flame.

▌ **A heater-rated electric fireplace** provides extra warmth and has an adjustable fan to regulate the temperature.

▌ **Remote controls** can turn on the power and adjust the flame speed and the heater fan.

**bright idea**

# more glow

Attract attention to your fireplace with romantic candle sconces, or install electric light sconces. Use shades to deflect glare, or install a dimmer.

**TOP LEFT** This model fits neatly into a corner and takes up little floor space.

**TOP RIGHT** At the push of a button, you can control the heat output and the flame patterns in this appliance.

**LEFT** Operable glass doors are one of the many options from which to choose.

**OPPOSITE** This electric fireplace and cabinet, which is available in several finishes, comes in one fully assembled package.

**LEFT** A remote control to regulate the fireplace offers added convenience in this bedroom.

**BELOW** If Victorian is your style, you can re-create the look with a model such as this one, which has been inserted into a faux-painted marble surround and mantel.

**OPPOSITE TOP** Heat can be turned on and off in most models, so you can enjoy the ambiance even during the warmest months of the year.

**OPPOSITE BOTTOM** This device has a built-in thermostate and an LED display with a delayed shutoff.

# electric fireplaces have come a long way

## **b**enefits

- Electric fireplaces can be economical to run. They use approximately the same amount of electricity as a standard incandescent lightbulb.
- You can run most electric fireplaces without the heater, so you can enjoy a "fire" comfortably year-round.
- At least one manufacturer makes an electric fireplace that has an integral air-filtering system that circulates and cleans the air in an average-size room with particulates and allergens as small as 1 micron. It runs four times per hour and comes with a washable (once a year) filter.

**bright idea**

*outdoor living*

Install an electric fireplace with a heater inside an enclosed porch. That's an economical way to extend your enjoyment of the space into the cooler months of the year.

# versatile and portable

**ABOVE** Display shelves on either side of this cabinet let the homeowner add a personal touch.

**LEFT** This electric fireplace features a furniture-like cabinet that includes drawers.

**OPPOSITE TOP** A set of strictly decorative tools adds a realistic note here.

**OPPOSITE BOTTOM LEFT** Brick-lined refractory sides within the firebox are made of sandstone.

**OPPOSITE BOTTOM RIGHT** A simple faux-marble surround adds elegance to this electric unit.

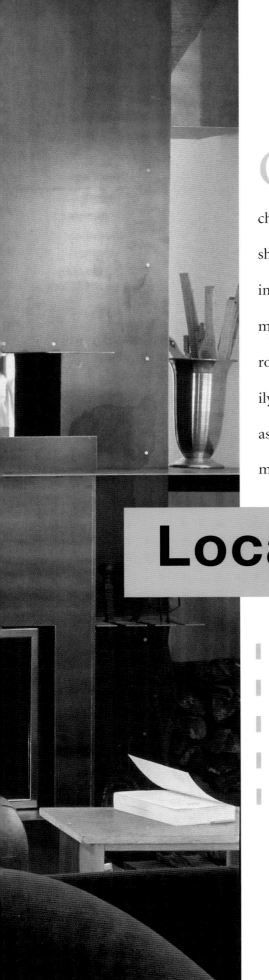

## 7

Grab a cup of coffee. Then find a comfortable chair, and sit back and relax. Take a tour of the following pages, which show how other homeowners have incorporated a fireplace or stove into various places in and around their homes. Current technology makes the installation of a hearth appliance possible in almost any room. Whether it's in the shared parts of the house—the living or family room, the kitchen, or an outdoor space—or the private areas, such as bedrooms or baths, a glowing fire can enhance your comfort on so many levels. Think about it. Then take your ideas to your installer.

# Location, Location

- indoors and outdoors
- places to gather
- kitchens
- baths and bedrooms
- healthy living in the great outdoors

Technology has improved the performance of a peninsula fireplace, which traditionally required a large volume of air to function properly.

**LEFT** Simply inviting—that's the feeling this Midwestern family room inspires, helped by a hearth that is accented with pretty blue and white tiles set in a checkerboard fashion.

**BELOW LEFT** In the Northeast, this patio is delightful from early spring through late fall, thanks to a new gas fireplace.

**RIGHT** A custom-built masonry fireplace adds architectural interest to this Southern California dining room.

# indoors and outdoors

Have you considered how a fireplace or stove could enhance your living room, the kitchen, master bedroom, or bath? A formal fireplace in the living room may be the perfect accent to the room's decor. A rustic design might suit the casual comfort of a family room or den. Is the kitchen the gathering place in your home? If so, perhaps that's where a fireplace may be enjoyed the most. You may want to consider a see-through design that allows shared fireplace privileges with an adjacent room, such as a dining room or outdoor-living area.

## living room comfort

**OPPOSITE** This large modern space does not lack warmth. The furnishings have been arranged to take advantage of the hearth—this living room's focal point.

**ABOVE** In an older, more traditional home, the fireplace adds architectural character to the room.

**RIGHT** A rugged stone fireplace anchors this eclectically decorated living room.

LEFT  A fireplace sets the cozy mood in this comfortable reading room.

ABOVE  The large brick hearth here suits the collection of American primitive furnishings and antiques.

RIGHT  A centrally located fireplace ties together two separate areas in this large great room. Matching the color of the fireplace's painted surround to the island buffet anchors the space.

## a desirable amenity

**ABOVE** It's easy to imagine the bride's party seated at this dining table toasting with glasses of champagne. When it's lit, the fireplace will make the room even more romantic.

**LEFT** You can roast hot dogs or marshmallows in this hand-built masonry fireplace that turns a patio into a fabulous outdoor-living room.

**RIGHT** A newly constructed vacation home has all the charm of much older structure, thanks in no small part to the fireplace that keeps this bedroom cozy even on cold winter nights.

The favorite gathering place in any home is usually the living or family room. It should reflect the personality and interests of the occupants. You might include collections, family photos, and mementoes in the decor and there may be a TV or a game table as well as other suitable furnishings. A fireplace can provide a welcoming ambiance in any part of the home where family and friends spend good times together.

# places to gather

Because these rooms are often used for entertainment purposes, a variety of fireplace options are available. A standard fireplace can be designed to stand out as a main focal point in the room and serve as an archor around which seating is arranged. See-through fireplaces and three-sided peninsula fireplaces are available to give you more arrangement options.

The mantel and overmantel provide space for displaying framed photographs, art, or other items that personalize the space. Change them with the seasons if you like. The important thing to remember is that this is where every member of the family should feel comfortable and guests welcomed. Hopefully, the lure of the fire will enhance those sentiments.

**BELOW** The soft glow of the fire can be enjoyed with others or alone.

**RIGHT** Draw furniture close to the fire before guests arrive to make the room feel intimate.

**OPPOSITE** In a new house, a fireplace wall serves as a partition between the living and dining areas of the open-plan design.

**ABOVE** In a recently renovated older home, walls came down to open up rooms that were once closed to each other. Here, the fireplace serves as a visual anchor between the dining and living rooms.

**RIGHT** A stone hearth suits this rustic yet refined dining room in a log house.

# kitchens

The kitchen is probably the most popular room in the majority of homes today. A lot of living happens here, from preparing meals to paying the bills, doing paperwork, crafting, and even entertaining guests. Some kitchens even feature dedicated entertainment centers. Now, many families are installing fireplaces for extra coziness or to provide visual relaxation at the beginning and end of a busy day. This is a particularly good idea if the kitchen is part of an open plan that includes the family or living room. So if you're thinking of remodeling your kitchen, you might want to consider adding a fireplace.

**LEFT** This reused space was taken down to expose the old brick, the fireplace, and the rafters, which add enormous vintage charm.

**OPPOSITE TOP** Tucked into a wall at the end of a run of cabinets, this fireplace can be enjoyed in both the work and dining areas of the kitchen.

**OPPOSITE BOTTOM** This river rock fireplace adds the right ingredient to make this country kitchen extra special.

Fireplaces and stoves can be installed just about anywhere today. Need a quick, temporary source of heat when you step out of the tub or shower? Install an electric or gas fireplace that provides ambiance and relaxation while soaking away the day's worries. Time to call it a night? What could be easier than using a remote control to create a fire for relaxation and romance. Ready to sleep? You don't even have to get out of bed. Just turn it off with the push of a button. Keep in mind, there are certain restrictions governing the use of hearth appliances in bathrooms and bedrooms, however. Check with your building department.

# baths and bedrooms

OPPOSITE A gas fireplace is a desirable amenity in a master bedroom that adds value to a house.

ABOVE This bedroom in a post-war apartment offers the luxury of its restored original masonry fireplace.

Sometimes an extra bedroom or bath may be located in a basement. A basement poses special challenges for natural-draft appliances. The perfect choice for basement installations is a direct-vent gas fireplace or a direct-vent gas stove. Because this type of fireplace has a sealed front and relies on combustion air for operation, it can be installed and function even in an airtight environment, such as a basement. If an existing basement, wood-burning fireplace smokes back into the room, a direct-vent gas insert can be installed, solving the problem. Another option would be to install a chimney fan to induce the draft. However, special provisions must be taken to ensure that it doesn't affect other natural-draft appliances such as a furnace or a water heater.

ABOVE  A kiva-style fireplace suits this bedroom in an adobe-style home in the Southwest.

**LEFT** A small fireplace in an older New England home adds a period touch to the bedroom. The painted mantel and paneled surround match the room's built-in storage.

**BELOW** This Victorian wood-burning fireplace is original to the house, although it has been refurbished to make it more energy efficient. If you plan to use an old fireplace, first have it inspected and serviced by a professional.

**bright idea**

## remote possibility

What's one more remote control? Adding a gas or electric fireplace with a remote control makes the fireplace easier to turn on and off and adjust, and because of that, will most likely be used more often.

## a personal spa

**ABOVE** Create a spectacular at-home retreat by installing a fireplace in the master bathroom.

**LEFT** By combining two small rooms, a homeowner was able to make a large master bath with luxurious amenities such as a fireplace.

**OPPOSITE** A fireplace and deep soaking tub—what could be more pampering?

**LEFT** The fireplace accents the grandness of this outdoor living room.

**BOTTOM LEFT** This opening serves as a bake oven. Once this unit gets to the proper temperature, homemade pies or pizzas can be baked.

**OPPOSITE** This limestone fireplace is an attractive outdoor focal point on a covered patio. The clay vessels set in the opening can be removed easily when a fire is desired.

# healthy living in the great outdoors

Outdoor living areas take advantage of nature and healthy living. Outdoor living rooms with fireplaces, fire pits, and barbeques are becoming a common place to entertain and spend family time throughout the warm-weather months and even beyond. Outdoor fireplaces are available in the traditional masonry for wood-burning applications. If convenience is important, gas fireplaces are designed with corrosion-resistant stainless-steel components. A simple economical alternative is a fire pit or chiminea. They are available as wood- or gas-fired units and they are portable, so you can move them to almost any area on a deck or patio.

## increased living space

OPPOSITE Outdoor dining can be enjoyed on this patio during the evening, even if it's a bit chilly, thanks to this stone fireplace.

ABOVE This outdoor living room was created by adding a covered patio adjacent to the exterior wall of this house. French doors on either side of the fireplace make moving easy between the interior and exterior spaces.

RIGHT Smoke stains above the opening of this porch fireplace can be scrubbed with a mixture of ½ cup of vinegar and a gallon of warm water. Use a firm bristle brush.

**OPPOSITE** A stainless-steel panel can be lowered to close the opening of this fireplace when it's not in use.

**ABOVE** This special area built on the back of a structure is the perfect private outdoor getaway.

**RIGHT** A unique, outdoor see-through fireplace provides enjoyable viewing from two sides.

**ABOVE** In an outdoor room designed for large family dinners and parties, the masonry fireplace provides heat on cool evenings.

**LEFT** This round fieldstone provides a rugged earthy backdrop for this cozy setting. The masonry fireplace is a custom design.

**OPPOSITE** A more refined design, this deck's soaring wood-burning fireplace has a cut-stone facade and chimney. The gray stone complements the home's shake siding that will weather naturally over time to a similar color.

## the last detail

# finishing finesse

**An outdoor room** is the perfect place for entertaining. So splurge a little, or a lot if you can afford it, on the way you finish your outdoor fireplace. A stone or tile facade can make your design special, even if the fireplace is a prefabricated unit.

ABOVE  Limestone 4 x 4 tiles set in a diamond pattern create interest on the face of this patio's wood-burning fireplace. The tiles match the larger limestone tiles that have been used on the patio floor.

OPPOSITE  Cut in an irregular pattern, here, the limestone that was used to finish this fireplace contrasts beautifully with the slate tiles that have been used on the floor of this outdoor room. A satin-finish nickel fireplace screen elevates the look to elegance.

**OPPOSITE** This unique fireplace is bedecked for the season.

**ABOVE** Part of an outdoor kitchen, this gas unit can be started by flipping the switch on the side panel.

**RIGHT** A summer lunch is set in front of an older wood-burning fireplace in this secret garden.

## 8

Make safety your number-one considera-tion when installing and using a fireplace or stove. Keep in mind that there will be an open flame in your house whether it's in the firebox or contained within the stove. Carefully research any company that you may hire to install or maintain of your system. Check that they have the necessary licenses, insurance, and certification. Ask for referrals. What is the company's reputation? After all, you are inviting these peo-ple into your home and literally trusting them with your life. You'll find other important safety information on the following pages.

# Safety Matters

| cautions | clearances and usage
| when sparks fly | chimneys

A video camera can be lowered into the chimney to deter-mine damage or fire risks, which could be lurking behind even this lovely fireplace.

Make sure your fireplace or woodstove has been tested and listed by a recognized source. It's only as safe as the appliance testing and the qualifications of the installing company. Ask for the owner's manual, which should specify the listing agency. Your manual will also provide installation information as well as advice regarding usage and maintenance of the appliance. Because specific skills and technical knowledge are required for the job, make sure that the installer is certified, whether your device is wood-burning or gas. Seek referrals and check credentials, too, which should be in writing. Also, the

# cautions

burning or gas. Seek referrals and check credentials, too, which should be in writing. Also, the National Fireplace Institute (NFI), a nonprofit, independent certification agency, can provide referrals in your area. Even if the installation is up to code, you are respnsible for using your fireplace or stove safely. You and your family can enjoy your hearth appliance, especially if you adhere to the proper recommended clearances, see to regular maintenance, and do all you can to prevent accidents.

**LEFT** It's important to always keep the spark screen closed when a fire is burning, although the bifold glass doors can remain open.

**OPPOSITE TOP** A standing spark screen is an important, yet functional accent piece.

**OPPOSITE BOTTOM LEFT** Make sure to have both the chimney and the appliance inspected annually and cleaned as needed.

**OPPOSITE BOTTOM RIGHT** Install a factory-built appliance according to the manufacturer instructions to make sure it conforms to its listing.

**LEFT** According to the National Fire Protection Standard 211, a chimney should be at least 3 ft. high and 2 ft. higher than any roof, building structure, or anything combustible within a 10-ft. horizontal distance.

**BELOW** Factory-built fireplaces have different clearance and listing requirements than masonry fireplaces. Always check the owner's manual.

**OPPOSITE TOP** A hearth extension must be of the proper thickness and extend in front of and to the sides of the fireplace as required by code.

**OPPOSITE BOTTOM** This firebox does not have a lining of fireclay brick, which is designed to withstand higher temperatures than conventional brick.

After the installation, you can still enjoy your fireplace without compromising your safety. Common sense should tell you that hanging holiday stockings too close to the fireplace opening can cause a disaster, but people do it. Omitting spark protection, log retainers, or placing furniture and other combustibles too close is also dangerous.

Don't avoid or put off fireplace and chimney maintenance, either. That can lead to a chimney fire or worse, a house fire. Make sure the chimney flue is clear and that there are no cracks in the masonry. You can do an annual inspection yourself, or leave it to a professional chimney sweep. Don't wait until fall. Some repairs take a while to complete, so it's best to have this job done during the mild-weather months.

The improper use of wood fireplaces and appliances—including the burning of trash or driftwood—will eventually lead to major expenses for repairs to your appliance, possibly fire damage to your home, and even the loss of life. This type of burning can cause excessive sparks or explosions. Even if you are careful about maintaining proper clearances, it may not be enough to keep you or your home safe under these circumstances.

A firescreen is essential. Also, using a fireplace hearth gate is an excellent way to keep children and adults from coming into direct contact with the fire or a hot stove.

# clearances and usage

Sparks can cause a fire inside a house in the same way that an unintentionally harmful bonfire can lead to an outdoor disaster. The best way to prevent sparking a fire in your house is to use spark-arresting products. At the top of the chimney, install a chimney cap with a spark arrestor to keep sparks off the roof. In some states, such as California, a ⅜-inch spark-arrestor screen is mandated. Check the regulations in your area. Indoors, always use an attached or standing spark screen with your wood- or gas-burning fireplace.

# when sparks fly

**TOP LEFT** This fireplace is not in use during the summer, but come fall, the owners will move the rug away from the opening so that they can enjoy a fire safely.

**TOP RIGHT** A single-wall black stovepipe requires a clearance of 18 in. from combustibles. Most double-wall black stovepipes have a 6- or 8-in. clearance requirement for the listing.

**LEFT** Electric and some gas appliances don't have as stringent code requirements as wood-burning fireplaces.

**OPPOSITE** Because wood and other materials can ignite when exposed to heat, it's important to always keep combustibles away from the fireplace when it's in use. This includes chairs, rugs, wood, or anything that can ignite.

The best way to prevent a fire is to examine the potential problems that could lead to one. Spark arrestors help keep sparks within the fireplace and from landing on roofs. Andirons help to hold the logs in the fireplace. Keeping combustibles the proper distance from the stove or fireplace is also a part of an owner's reponsibility. However, there are things that can't always be anticipated, which is why it's so important to install smoke and carbon monoxide alarms in your home. A chimney that hasn't been cleaned recently can lead to a chimney fire. An obstructed chimney can push carbon monoxide from a vented gas-log set back into the room. A hidden beam installed as part of the chimney can ignite.

Many times, the only way to detect a problem is with a chimney video-inspection camera. A professional might also want to open up the chimney. If a qualified chimney professional feels this must be done, believe it. However, a second opinion is always an option. There are three levels of inspection mentioned in the National Fire Prevention Association Standard 211, which outlines when the next level of inspection must be taken.

# chimneys

**BOTTOM LEFT** Even though the hearth is raised off the floor, it still has specific outer-hearth, floor-protection requirements.

**BOTTOM RIGHT** Never use flammable liquids to start a fire. Many have flashpoints whereby combustible fumes that flash back to the fume source (liquid) can cause an explosion and fire.

**RIGHT** A fireplace opening that is smaller than 6 sq. ft. requires a hearth extension that is at least 16 in. in front of the facing. A fireplace that is 6 sq. ft. or larger must have at least a 20-in. hearth extension.

**OPPOSITE BOTTOM LEFT** If you suspect that a gas log set has a leak, leave the house and call the gas company or fire department from a neighbor's home.

**OPPOSITE BOTTOM RIGHT** When a fireplace is properly constructed, it's still only as safe as the person who uses and maintains it.

# Resource Guide

**Aladdin Hearth Products**

Phone: 800-234-2508

Fax: 800-546-4474

1445 North Hwy.

Colville, WA 99114-2008

www.quadrafire.com

*Manufactures the Quadra-Fire line of home heating systems that include clean-burning hearth appliances, freestanding stoves, gas fireplaces, and gas, wood, and pellet inserts.*

**Aloha Fireplaces**

7655 E. Evans Rd.

Scottsdale, AZ 85260

Phone: 480-922-1042

www.alohafireplace.com

*Specializes in custom fireplaces, fireplace tile, and accessories.*

**American Gas Association (AGA)**

400 N. Capital St. N.W.

Washington, DC 20001

Phone: 202-824-7000

Fax: 202-824-7115

www.aga.org

*Represents 189 local natural gas utilities. These companies deliver gas to 54 million businesses and homes all across the United States. AGA offers information for the consumer about energy efficiency and appliances.*

**Buckley Rumford Fireplaces**

1035 Monroe St.

Port Townsend, WA 98368

Phone: 360-385-9974

www.rumford.com

*A source for Rumford fireplaces, fireplace parts and other related products, and dealers.*

**California Redwood Association**

405 Enfrente Dr.

Novato, CA 94949

Phone: 415-382-0662

www.calred.org

*The trade association for redwood lumber producers. It offers design advice and redwood lumber sources.*

**Central Fireplace**

20502 160th St.

Greenbush, MN 56726

The following list of manufacturers and associations is meant to be a general guide to additional industry and product-related sources. It is not intended as a listing of products and manufacturers represented by the photographs in this book.

Phone: 800-248-4681

Fax: 218-782-2580

www.centralfireplace.com

*Manufactures gas fireplaces, freestanding stoves, gas inserts, and child-proof remote controls.*

## C.J.'s Home Decor & Fireplaces

120 Stryker Ln., Suite 209

Hillsborough, NJ 08844

Phone: 888-986-1535

Fax: 908-904-1575

www.fireplacesandgrills.com

*Sells and installs grill and hearth products for indoor and outdoor use.*

## Cumberland Woodcraft Company

P.O. Drawer 609

Carlisle, PA 17013-0609

Phone: 717-243-0063

www.cumberlandwoodcraft.com

*A retailer of handcrafted Victorian-style fireplace mantels, corbels, bars, millwork, and hardwood carvings among other things.*

## Dancing Fire, Inc.

Phone: 817-613-0029

Fax: 817-594-0039

www.dancingfire.com

*A company specializing in the sale of chimineas and Pinion firewood, which is ideal for aromatic chiminea fires.*

## Duraflame, Inc.

P.O. Box 1230

Stockton, CA 95201

Phone: 800-342-2896

Fax: 209-462-9412

www.duraflame.com

*Makes firelogs, fire-starters, and related accessories for indoor and outdoor fireplaces.*

## Endless Summer Patio Heaters

Phone: 800-762-1142

Fax: 847-731-6032

www.uniflame.com/patio_heaters/

*Sells residential, commercial, and tabletop heaters for outdoor use. The company also sells outdoor wood-burning fireplaces. Endless Summer is an affiliate of The UniFlame Corporation.*

# Resource Guide

**Final Touches**
115 Morris St.
Blowing Rock, NC 28605
Phone: 877-506-2741
www.chiminea.net
*A retailer of chimineas and related accessories.*

**Fire Designs**
310 N. Michigan Ave.
Suite 200
Chicago, IL 60601-3702
Phone: 800-661-4788
Fax: 312-263-5855
www.firedesigns.net
*Manufactures fireplace-related products.*

**Fires of Tradition**
17 Passmore Crescent
Brantford, ON
Canada N3T 5L6
Phone: 519-770-0063
www.firesoftradition.com
*Sells fireplace accessories, baskets, castings, ceramic surrounds, hearths, mantels, and electric, gas, and wood-burning fireplaces.*

**Heat-N-Glo**
20802 Kensington Blvd.
Lakeville, MN 55044
Phone: 888-743-2887
Fax: 800-259-1549
www.heatnglo.com
*Manufactures a wide range of gas and wood-burning fireplaces, log sets, and fireplace inserts.*

**The Hearth, Patio, and Barbecue Association (HPBA)**
1601 N. Kent St., Suite 1001
Arlington, VA 22209
Phone: 703-522-0086
Fax: 703-522-0548
http://hpba.org
*Established to promote the hearth products industry in North America. Members include distributors, manufacturers, non-profit organizations, associates, retailers, and service companies.*

**Hearthlink Outdoor Fireplaces**
9 Maple St.
Randolph, VT 05060
Phone: 877-337-8414
Fax: 802-728-4809
www.outdoorfireplaces.com
*A source for cast-aluminum chimineas and fireplaces.*

## Heatilator Products

1915 W. Saunders

Mt. Pleasant, IA 52641

Phone: 800-843-2848

Fax: 800-248-2038

www.heatilator.com

*Offers a broad line of gas, electric, and wood-burning fireplaces, as well as fireplace inserts, gas logs, and outdoor fireplace products.*

## J.A. Getz Company

8616 S. 228th St.

Kent, WA 98031

Phone: 253-850-0466

Fax: 253-850-0469

www.jagetz.com

*Sells mantels in a variety of decorative and architectural styles.*

## Lennox Hearth Products

1110 W. Taft Ave.

Orange, CA 92865-4150

www.lennoxhearthproducts.com

*Makes fireplaces, stoves, inserts, and gas logs.*

## Majestic Vermont Castings Stoves

www.majesticgaslogs.com

*Manufactures indoor and outdoor gas and wood-burning fireplaces, freestanding stoves, and accessories.*

## Mantels of Yesteryear

P.O. Box 908

McCaysville, GA 30555

Phone: 706-492-5534

Fax: 706-492-3758

www.mantelsofyesteryear.com

*Manufactures and sells to the consumer reproduction fireplace mantels in many styles. Delivery is nationwide.*

## Martin Gas Products

Martin Gas Industries, Inc.

301 E. Tennessee St.

Florence, AL 35630

Phone: 866-244-0750

Fax: 256-740-5192

www.martingas.com

*Manufactures fireplaces, fireplace inserts, and gas heaters with different venting options. The company also sells related hearth products. The Web site provides a dealer locator. Martin Gas Products is a division of Martin Gas Industries, Inc.*

# Resource Guide

**Miles Industries/ Valor**

829 W. Third St.

N. Vancouver, BC

Canada V7P 3K7

Phone: 800-468-2567

Fax: 604-984-0246

www.valorflame.com

*Sells natural gas fireplaces and fireplace inserts that match classic firebox dimensions. The Web site provides dealer information and an online Btu calculator for determining Btu requirements.*

**Mountain Stream Forge**

P.O. Box 262

Canby, OR 97013

Phone: 800-392-4604

Fax: 503-263-6329

www.mountainstreamforge.com

*Makes hand-forged, iron fireplace accessories and equipment.*

**National Chimney Sweep Guild**

2155 Commercial Dr.

Plainfield, IN 46168

Phone: 317-837-1500

Fax: 317-837-5365

www.ncsg.org

*Provides local chimney sweep referrals nationwide.*

**Raytech, Inc**

2 Fallbrook

Irvine, CA 92604

Phone: 800-838-5898

Fax: 949-653-1030

www.raytechstore.com

*Offers an array of fireplace products, including tools, patio heaters, mantels, and wood stoves.*

**Regency Fireplace Products**

www.regencyshowcase.com

*Manufactures gas-fueled and wood-burning fireplaces and stoves, as well as fireplace inserts. The Regency Web site allows the customer to create and design a personal fireplace look, and to find the nearest dealer.*

**Superior Fireplaces**

1110 W. Taft Ave.

Orange, CA 92865

www.lennoxhearthproducts.com

*Manufactures fireplaces. Superior is affiliated with*

*Lennox Hearth Products. The Web site provides a list of dealers.*

**Temco Fireplace Products**
1190 W. Oleander
Perris, CA 92571
Phone: 909-657-7311
Fax: 909-943-1841
www.temcofireplaces.com
*Manufactures gas and wood-burning fireplace products. The Web site provides a list of distributors.*

**Tulikivi U.S. Inc.**
One Penn Plaza, Suite 3600
New York, NY 10119
Phone: 212-896-3897
Fax: 212-760-1088
www.tulikivi.com
*Manufactures stoves, cookstoves, and fireplaces.*

**UniFlame Corporation**
1817 N. Kenosha Rd.
Zion, IL 60099
Phone: 800-762-1142
Fax: 847-731-6032

www.uniflame.com
*Specializes in outdoor patio heaters, fireplace accessories, and barbecue grills.*

**Vermont Castings**
410 Admiral Blvd.
Mississauga, ON
Canada L5T 2N6
Phone: 800-668-5323
Fax: 877-565-2929
www.vermontcastings.com
*Manufactures hearth and heating products including gas, wood-burning, and electric stoves and fireplaces.*

**Waterford Irish Stoves**
www.waterfordstoves.com
*Makes porcelain enamel, cast-iron wood-burning stoves and wood-burning and gas fireplaces. The Web site offers tips for heating with gas and wood, answers questions related to hearth products, and contains a listing of dealers.*

# Glossary

**Adobe fireplace:** A fireplace representative of American Southwest architecture, made of sun-dried brick and generally found in hot climates.

**Andiron:** A metal-crafted log support with a decorative vertical shaft. It is attached to a horizontal bar mounted on short legs.

**Art Deco:** A design movement that started in France and became popular in the United States during the 1920s and 1930s. It is characterized by geometric forms, zig-zags, inlays, and lacquer finishes.

**Art Nouveau:** A late-nineteenth-century style that rejects historical references and uses organic forms and sinuous stylized curves as decoration.

**Arts and Crafts:** A design movement led by architect William Morris in England during the late nineteenth century. It rejected industrialization and encouraged the use of natural materials and hand-craftsmanship. It soon gained popularity in the United States, where it is also called Craftsman style.

**Ash dump:** An enclosed system that allows for clearing ash from the hearth and emptying it into an ash pit, which is located beneath the firebox.

**Asymmetry:** The balance between objects of different sizes as the result of placement or grouping.

**Balance:** The equilibrium among forms in a room or on a surface. Balanced relationships between objects can be either symmetrical or asymmetrical.

**Baroque:** An exaggerated, heavily ornamented, theatrical seventeenth-century European decorative style that features oversized curves, twisted columns, broken pediments, and large-scale moldings.

**Btu:** The abbreviation for British thermal unit; a standard measurement of heat energy.

**Cape Cod lighter:** A small metal pot with a pumice ball on a metal wand. It's used with kerosene as a fire-starter.

**Catalytic combustor:** A ceramic device that lowers the temperature at which smoke will ignite and burn. A chute directs smoke to a combustion chamber where the combustor burns off particulates.

**Ceramic firebox:** A firebox engineered of modern refractory materials that makes a fire burn cleaner, hotter, and more efficiently.

**Chiminea:** An outdoor fire device that originated in seventeenth-century Mexico as a clay oven for baking bread. Today, both traditional clay as well as sturdy metal chimineas are available.

**Chimney:** The part of the fireplace that transports smoke and other byproducts of the burning fire upward through the roof and into the atmosphere.

**Damper:** A movable device resembling a plate that spans the lower end of the smoke chamber and opens or closes the fireplace flue.

**Damper hanger:** A device that hooks onto the end of the damper to show that the damper is closed.

**Damper plaque:** A small plaque that flips up or down to indicate when the fireplace damper is open or closed, respectively.

**Fatwood:** Wood cut from pine stumps containing a high amount of flammable resin, sold as a fire-starter.

**Federal:** Early nineteenth-century American decorative and architectural style, closely resembling that of the English

Georgian period. Highly symmetrical, it features classical and patriotic motifs.

**Fireback:** A vertical metal accessory placed behind the fire to absorb heat and radiate it back into the room.

**Fireboard:** A decorative covering that can be placed in front of the opening when the fireplace is not in use.

**Firebox:** The part of the fireplace that contains the burning fuel and fire. It is also referred to as the fire chamber.

**Fire pit:** A wood-, gas-, or alcohol gel-fueled device used for outdoor fires. It can be made of metal (portable) or custom-built using masonry (permanent).

**Fire-starter logs:** A treated block of sawdust and wax used to start a fire.

**Flue:** The passageway that transports the byproducts of burning fuel to the outside atmosphere.

**Georgian:** A predominantly eighteenth-century English architecture and furniture style that is ele-gant, symmetrical, and classical in form. It was in-spired by the excavations of ancient sites in Greece and Pompeii.

**Harmony:** The coherence of different design elements achieved by color, shape, or motif.

**Hearth:** The floor of the firebox. It some-times extends into the room.

**Hearth rug:** A protection for the floor made of wool, which is naturally fire-resistant, or synthetic materials treated with flame-retardant chemicals.

**Line:** In design terms, line defines space. Different lines (vertical, horizontal, diago-nal, curved) denote various qualities.

**Lintel:** The horizontal support spanning the top opening at the front of the firebox.

**Mantel:** The shelf that is mounted above the fireplace opening and across the face.

**Noncatalytic stove:** A stove built with a second chamber outside the firebox where smoke is directed.

**Patio heater:** An outdoor heating source usually consisting of a heater within a dome. Most patio heaters provide heat within a 15- to 20-foot radius.

**Proportion:** The relationship of parts or objects to one another based on size.

**Rhythm:** In design terms, moving the eye around a room at a measured pace set up by repeating motifs, colors, or shapes.

**Rococo:** Predominently French and Ger-man eighteenth-century decorative move-ment that reacted to classicism. It features elaborately carved naturalistic forms such as flora and fauna.

**Scale:** The size of something as it relates to the size of everything else around it.

**Smoke chamber:** The area between the damper and the opening of the flue.

**Smoke shelf:** The floor at the back of the smoke chamber.

**Surround:** The facing ornamentation on the sides and top of the fireplace opening.

**Symmetry:** The identical arrangement of objects, forms, or parts on both sides of a centerline.

**Throat:** The narrow opening aiding the flow of smoke, gas, and flames into the smoke chamber and out through the chimney.

# Index

# Index

# Photo Credits

All photos by Jessie Walker with the following exceptions: **page 1:** Alhambra **page 3:** Mark Lohman **page 4:** Joseph DeLeo **page 38:** *top left* Nancy Hill/Deborah Lipner LTD Interiors, *top right* Mark Samu/Rinaldi Associates, *bottom* Mark Lohman/William Hefner **page 39:** Beth Singer **page 43:** *top* Thomas McConnell **page 47:** *bottom left* Sonoma Stone, *bottom right* Tuliviki Stone **page 48:** *top* coutesy of Brickoff Design Associates **page 49:** Tuliviki Stone **page 50:** *both* Tuliviki Stone **page 52:** Mark Lohman **page 53:** *bottom right* Mark Lohman **page 54:** *top* Mark Lohman, *bottom* Hearth & Home **page 55:** *top right* Eric Roth, *bottom* Hearth & Home **page 56:** *top left* Karyn Millet, *top right* Mark Lohman, *bottom* Thomas McConnell **page 58:** Mark Samu **page 71:** Boulder Creek **page 77:** *both* Chesney's Inc. **page 79:** *both* Chesney's Inc. **page 92:** *top* Hearth & Home **page 93:** *bottom* Hearth & Home **page 95:** *top right* davidduncanlivingston.com **page 98:** Beth Singer **page 100:** Bob Greenspan/Susan Andrews, stylist **page 101:** *top & bottom right* Mark Lohman, *bottom left* davidduncanlivingston.com **page 102:** *top* Eric Roth, *bottom* davidduncanlivingston.com **page 104:** *bottom* Hearth & Home **page 105:** *bottom* Hearth &

Home **page 106:** *bottom left* Todd Caverly, bottom right Mark Lohman **page 107:** *top* Eric Roth, *bottom left* Mark Lohman, *bottom right* davidduncanlivingston.com **page 108:** *to* davidduncanlivingston.com, *bottom* Thomas McConnell **page 109:** top davidduncanlivingston.com, *bottom* Mark Lohman **page 110:** davidduncanlivingston.com **page 111:** *top and bottom left* Mark Lohman, *bottom right* davidduncanlivingston.com **page112:** davidduncanlivingston.com **page 113:** *top left* Chesney's Inc., *top right* davidduncanlivingston.com, *bottom* Mark Lohman **page 116:** *bottom left* Vermont Castings **page 117:** *top* Vermont Castings. *bottom right* Mark Samu **page 118:** *bottom* Vermont Castings **page 120:** *bottom* Vermont Castings **page 121:** *both* Vermont Castings **page 122:** *bottom* Vermont Castings **page 124:** Mark Samu **page 125:** *top left* Vermont Castings **page 126:** *top* Mark Samu **page 127:** *top right & bottom* Tria Giovan **page 129:** *top left* Mark Samu, *top right* Vermont Castings **page 130:** Vermont Castings **page 131:** *top* Mark Samu, *bottom both* Vermont Castings **page 132-137:** *all* Vermont Castings **page 138:** davidduncanlivingston.com **page 140-141:** *top & bottom left* Vermont Castings, *bottom right* Linex **page 142** both

Vermont Castings **page 143:** *top* Vermont Castings, *bottom* Linex **page 144:** *top* Linex **page 145:** *top left* Vermont Castings, *top right & bottom* Hearth & Home **page 146:** *top left & bottom* Hearth & Home, *top right* Vermont Castings **page 147:** Vermont Castings **page 148:** *top* Hearth & Home, *bottom* Mark Samu **page 149:** *top* Vermont Castings, *bottom* Hearth & Home page 150: *bottom right* Hearth & Home **page 151:** *bottom left* Vermont Castings, *bottom right* Linex **page 152:** Minh + Wass **page 154:** *bottom* Hearth & Home **page 155:** Tria Giovan **page 156:** Joseph DeLeo **page 160:** Mark Lohman **page 162:** Alhambra **page 163:** Retna **page 164:** Mark Lohman **page 165:** *top* Eric Roth **page 166:** Tria Giovan **page 169:** Eric Roth **page 172:** Mark Lohman **page 173:** Eric Roth **page 174:** *both* Tria Giovan **page 175:** Mark Lohman **page 176:** Mark Lohman **page 177:** Tria Giovan **page 178:** Tria Giovan **page 179:** *top* Mark Lohman, *bottom* Tria Giovan **page 180:** *top* Tria Giovan, *bottom* Mark Lohman **page 181:** Eric Roth **page 182:** bottom Tria Giovan, *bottom* Hearth & Home **page 183:** Karyn Millet **page 185:** *top* Hearth & Home, *bottom* Tony Giammarino

# If you like
# Design Ideas for Fireplaces,
take a look at the rest of the
# Design Idea series

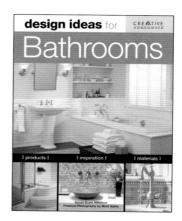